ART
INC.

ART
INC.

The Essential Guide for Building
Your Career as an Artist

Lisa Congdon

Edited by Meg Mateo Ilasco
Foreword by Jonathan Fields

CHRONICLE BOOKS
SAN FRANCISCO

Library of Congress Cataloging-in-Publication Data available.

ISBN 978-1-4521-2826-9

Manufactured in China.

MIX
Paper from
responsible sources
FSC
www.fsc.org   FSC® C016973

Designed by Meg Mateo Ilasco.

American Illustration is a registered trademark of American Illustration, Inc. Anthropologie is a registered trademark of U.O. Merchandise Inc. Apple is a registered trademark of Apple Inc. Big Cartel is a registered trademark of Indie Labs, LLC. Bit.ly is a registered trademark of Bitly, Inc. Blogger is a registered trademark of Haumann Smal Design Studio. Canon is a registered trademark of Canon Kabushiki Kaisha Corporation. Cardstore.com is a registered trademark of Cardstore.Com, Inc. Craigslist is a registered trademark of craigslist, Inc. Epson is a registered trademark of Seiko Epson Kabushiki Kaisha Corporation Limited. Etsy is a registered trademark of Etsy, Inc. Excel is a registered trademark of Microsoft Corp. Facebook is a registered trademark of Facebook, Inc. Flickr is a registered trademark of Yahoo! Inc. Ford is a registered trademark of Ford Motor Company Corporation. Fossil is a registered trademark of Fossil Group, Inc. Freelancers Union is a registered trademark of Freelancers Union, Inc. FreshBooks is a registered trademark of 2ndSite Inc. Google is a registered trademark of Google Inc. Hewlett-Packard is a registered trademark of Hewlett-Packard Development Company, L.P. Imagekind is a registered trademark of Imagekind, Inc. Instagram is a registered trademark of Instagram, LLC. iPad is a registered trademark of Apple Inc. iPhoto is a registered trademark of Apple Inc. Kashoo is a registered trademark of Kashoo Inc. Kinko's is a registered trademark of Federal Express Corporation. Madison Park Greetings is a registered trademark of Madison Park Greetings, Inc. Makerie is a registered trademark of The Makerie Limited Liability Company. New York Times is a registered trademark of The New York Times Company. Papyrus is a registered trademark of Schurman Fine Papers Corporation. Paypal is a registered trademark of PayPal, Inc. Peachtree is a registered trademark of Sage Software, Inc. Pendleton Woolen Mills is a registered trademark of Pendleton Woolen Mills, Inc. Photoshop is a registered trademark of Adobe Systems Inc. Picasa is a registered trademark of Google Inc. Pinterest is a registered trademark of Cold Brew Labs, Inc. PrintSource is a registered trademark of PrintSource Corporation. QuickBooks is a registered trademark of Intuit, Inc. Saatchi Online is a registered trademark of Saatchi Online, Inc. Shopify is a registered trademark of Jaded Pixel Technologies, Inc. Society6 is a registered trademark of Demand Media, Inc. Surtex is a registered trademark of George Little Management, Inc. Target is a registered trademark of Target Brands, Inc. TinyURL is a registered trademark of DIOB LLC. Todoist is a registered trademark of Doist limited company. Tumblr is a registered trademark of Tumblr, Inc. Twitter is a registered trademark of Twitter, Inc. Typepad is a registered trademark of Six Apart Ltd. Urban Outfitters is a registered trademark of Urban Outfitters, Inc. Virb is a registered trademark of Media Temple, Inc. Wite-Out is a registered trademark of Wite-Out Products, Inc. WordPress is a registered trademark of Automattic Inc. Workbook is a registered trademark of Jupitermedia Corporation. X-acto is a registered trademark of Elmer's Products, Inc.

10 9 8 7 6 5 4 3 2 1

Chronicle Books LLC
680 Second Street
San Francisco, California 94107
www.chroniclebooks.com

To my mother, Gerrie,
for showing me it's never too late
to find your bliss.

CONTENTS

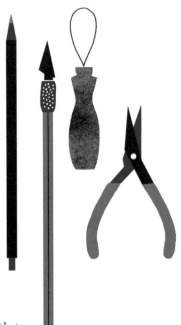

FOREWORD

Art and business? In the same sentence?! What are you . . . nuts?! Maybe yes, maybe no. There is so much mythology, judgment, and suffering around the idea of art and money.

When I was a kid, my mom was a gifted potter. One wall of the basement was lined with rows of industrial shelves weighed down by hundreds of mysterious powder-filled mason jars labeled things like "Celadon," "China Red," or "Low Fire." A prehistoric-looking kick-wheel anchored the space, boasting a two-hundred-pound concrete flywheel that took out shins of unaware passersby on a regular basis. Then came the four electric wheels and a cacophony of tools that allowed for high-speed manhandling in the name of art.

On the weekends, we would pack up the Ford Custom van and head off to a local outdoor street fair or market to sell the week's wares. I can't remember a time when we weren't surrounded by artisans and craftspeople, from weavers and glassblowers to painters and sculptors.

So it wasn't unusual when, in my early teens, I propped an old door on some clay boxes at the far end of the studio, clamped on an old swing-arm light, grabbed my grandfather's acrylics, and began to paint. And paint. And paint. As soon as I was good enough, I started hustling gigs painting album covers on jean jackets in exchange for walking-around money.

Though I've traded paint for words and denim for paper, I've lived, breathed, and been surrounded by the process of creation for as long as I can remember. What's so interesting is, as a kid, the notion of any tension between art and money simply didn't exist. I loved to create. I worked to become decent at it. People paid me to do it. Simple as that.

But, for some reason, when you hit a certain age and a certain level of "seriousness," and you start calling yourself an "artist," making a living at it becomes a source of great controversy. People who have nothing to do with the exchange between you and those who would enjoy your work start to pass judgment. Money, they proclaim, bastardizes both the process and the output.

Why this cultural rift emerged, I really don't know. Maybe it has to do with the establishment of a power and money structure defined largely by gatekeepers and chosen ones—external arbiters controlling the flow of not only eyeballs, but income. Maybe it comes from the ire of those who've not yet figured out how to make their calling their profession seeking to tear down those who have, labeling them sellouts and hacks. Maybe it stems from something entirely different.

Whatever the source, what's become clear to me is that you no longer have to wait to be picked.

While the traditional path to love and money in art is still alive and well, the last ten years have seen the emergence of an extraordinary array of alternative paths. Those that allow you to eschew the traditional gatekeepers and go straight to the buyers. Those that empower you to stake a claim to your own global digital gallery space and generate a legion of raving fans. Those that fuel your ability to build and generate a real living, serving everyone from collectors to consumers and even large organizations. And the best part is, you often don't have to find them; they'll find you.

There's no better example than my friend, illustrator, artist, and author Lisa Congdon. Lisa was anything but a "born artist." In fact, she came to art later in life with very little formal training. Yet, in a matter of years, she built not only an astonishing body of work, but the ability to earn a very nice full-time income making art. No side gigs. No occasional shift at the local pub. No excuses. She makes art. All day. Every day.

Lisa wakes up and does what she loves. A lot of what she loves. So much that she's become exceptional at it. And she makes a living doing it.

Exactly how she made this happen, and how you can, too, is what *Art Inc.* is all about.

Jonathan Fields

INTRODUCTION

When I was growing up, I didn't have any plans to be an artist. I made drawings and paintings at school, but art was not something I thought I was good at. So art, as a living, had never entered my mind. Fast-forward to 2001: at the age of thirty-two, I picked up a paintbrush for the first time since the sixth grade. At the time, I was working as a project manager at a nonprofit organization, and I had just ended an eight-year relationship. I was looking for a distraction, so I signed up for a painting class at a local university's extension program, brought some blank canvases home, and started painting. There, in the privacy of my apartment, I began a journey that I never could have imagined would lead me into the life I live today.

In part because of that simple decision, I went from being someone with no art experience and a very basic skill set to someone who now has a full-time career drawing and painting. Prior to taking that art class, I had no idea what creative abilities were hidden inside me. And, for the record, talent didn't exactly pour out of me instantly. Curiosity, determination, and hard work played a huge role in my development.

What felt different about art from former pursuits was that I was motivated by something new: an intrinsic desire to create. It was deep-seated and primal; I had to make art like I had to breathe. From this passion came a desire to expand my skills, even in areas that were out of my comfort zone. I taught myself to use new media and techniques and practiced for hours and hours until my hand felt like it would fall off.

In 2005, I began sharing my work online on platforms like Flickr and Blogger. Soon I was connecting with people who would eventually buy my work, offer me shows in galleries, and remain my friends and collaborators today. Later, as social media and online sales platforms exploded, I began using the Internet in more concerted and strategic ways to build community, promote and sell my work, and build a client base.

Eventually all of my work paid off. I reached a point where I was making a steady full-time living as an artist. I began to think about how I got to this tipping point and how other artists were making it happen, too. While there is no one perfect formula that will work for every artist, I realized there are a few clear paths and work habits that, used in some combination, can lead to consistent, paying, and satisfying work. In this book, I'll talk primarily about the paths of fine art sales, commissions, print sales, illustration, and licensing, and how you can use them in different combinations to create your own personal blueprint for success.

It's important to remember that success isn't just financial—getting checks and paying your bills is important, but it's not everything. You can define your own benchmarks for success. But no matter how savvy you are at achieving your goals or making money, unless you are creating art and selling it in ways that resonate with your values and core aesthetic, you will likely be miserable as an artist. In the pages to come, I will share methods for finding your voice and niche so that you can feel good about your choices and stay connected to your creative process.

Throughout the book, I'll also share many of my own experiences, along with the stories of other artists who are making a full-time living. I'll cover a range of topics central to building and sustaining a successful art business: developing your authentic voice, organizing your business, promoting your work, using social media, finding income streams that work for you, and managing the ebb and flow of your career. This book is designed to support artists at all points in their careers—whether you are a new artist who just discovered your talent, a part-time artist who wants to accelerate into making art full-time, or a seasoned artist looking for new ideas to stimulate your existing career.

You may be asking, "It might be possible for others, but is it possible for me?" The answer is a matter of determination. While there have certainly been a few inexplicable, magical moments in my career, most of what has gotten me to where I am today are more basic things like curiosity, patience, risk-taking, and hard work. As you read about the artists interviewed in this book, you'll see that it's true for them as well. So while establishing yourself solidly in the art market might take time, the good news is that it is almost always the result of concrete action and not simple luck. With this book, you'll have the guidance and information you need to turn your artistic talents into a thriving career. With effort and dedication, you'll no doubt make your dream a reality.

YOU *are* AN ARTIST

I am always delighted when I hear stories of artists using their talents to become entrepreneurs, and it's something that happens more and more every day. No wonder: artists are some of the world's most innovative thinkers, and many are redefining what it means to be an artist, to sell work, and to be successful.

One thing I know for sure is that to be a successful artist, you must start with the simplest proclamation: I am an artist. It's a basic assertion, but seeing yourself as an artist—legitimate and genuine—can be transformational. This chapter is about just that: embracing your identity as an artist and believing you can thrive in the profession. In this chapter, you'll learn how to tackle doubts, find your voice, make time and a space to work, and announce your aspirations to the world—critical prerequisites to starting your art business.

EMBRACING YOURSELF AS AN ARTIST

Embracing yourself as an artist is the first significant step on the path toward building your career. It's not always an easy step to take. When you affirm yourself as an artist, the road before you can feel equally exciting and terrifying. It can be thrilling when you are moving toward fulfilling your dream and spending time doing something you truly love. On the flip side, doubt can rear its ugly head, causing you to question if this profession can really pay the bills or whether you're talented enough.

As you'll see in the profile interviews, many artists experience a tension between wanting to make art their livelihood and believing it is possible. But every single one of them learned through their experience that being an artist is a viable career choice. In fact, because of the potential of the Internet, there are more opportunities today for working artists than have ever existed before. Artists have access to marketplaces like Etsy and shopping platforms like Big Cartel to sell their work. And getting your work out there and noticed has been made easier by social media platforms like Twitter, Facebook, Pinterest, and the like.

If you feel anxious about your talent, it's important to understand that almost all artists experience insecurity at some point in their careers—and often throughout their careers. Maybe you don't feel worthy of success because you haven't attended art school or because you're starting your career later in life. Maybe you feel apprehensive because you aren't sure your work is good enough. But just remember that established, successful artists were once in your shoes, too. It's important to not let these fears seize your productivity or your will to work.

Indeed, doubt and insecurity are feelings that can paralyze us and hinder creativity if we allow them. But when artists begin to think of their work in a more positive light, doors open and

> *When you affirm yourself as an artist, the road before you can feel equally exciting and terrifying.*

success follows. Simply telling yourself, "I can do this," or, "This *is* possible," works wonders. And remember that the first few years of an artist's career—being the new kid on the block—is actually a really magical and memorable time. So enjoy it.

THE THRIVING ARTIST'S MIND-SET

Much of what separates successful artists from those who struggle is simply their mind-set. Struggling artists often create obstacles in their minds by making erroneous assumptions about the way the world works. They give weight to the "starving artist myth"—part conventional belief that pursuing a career as an artist leads to financial struggle and part romanticized notion that art is better when created in a state of deprivation. But the starving artist myth is just that: a myth. And believing in any part of it will keep you from becoming a thriving, working artist.

Creating a flourishing art practice comes from passion, talent, and hard work. Promoting your work means that people will know what you do. And selling your work will support your livelihood and allow you to make even more art. This is the "thriving artist's mind-set." Artists who possess this mentality are not frightened by the notion of making money. They think in terms of possibility and abundance, not limits and scarcity. They've given themselves permission to thrive.

Shifting Your Mind-Set

Which mind-set do you possess: that of a starving artist or a thriving artist? Read the chart on the following page and see in which category your thoughts about pursuing an art career belong.

Starving Artist's Mind-Set	*Thriving Artist's Mind-Set*
"Focusing on how to make money from my art prevents me from making good work."	"Putting effort toward making a living from my art allows me to do what I love."
"Good art markets and sells itself; I shouldn't have to actively promote my work."	"I proudly and actively share my art and talent with the world. Doing this helps my work to sell so I can make a living."
"The only way to be successful as an artist is to get into a really good gallery."	"There is no single 'perfect' way to be a successful artist. I will allow myself to explore and discover new creative avenues I might also enjoy."
"Having little money and suffering for my art will make me a better artist."	"Making good work comes from passion, talent, and hard work."

If most of your thoughts were aligned with the starving artist's mind-set, there's no need to be worried. There are practical things you can do to move from fear to action. First, pay attention to the negative messages you tell yourself about what is possible and write them down. Next, shift the messages by changing pessimistic statements to more positive ones. Surround yourself with people, including other artists, who support your aspirations and dreams. Supportive friends, family, and mentors can serve as inspiration for what is possible. Last, work to find your voice as an artist. Finding your voice will help you build confidence that will carry you through times of doubt. Understanding and appreciating your own unique perspective as an artist will contribute enormously to your motivation, work ethic, and sense of potential.

NIKKI MCCLURE

Papercut artist

OLYMPIA, WASHINGTON

WWW.NIKKIMCCLURE.COM

If you take a look at Nikki McClure's intricate and beautiful papercut art, you might have her pegged for an art school graduate. You probably wouldn't have guessed that she is self-taught and her road to becoming an artist actually started in the ecology department of her college. The inspiration to become an artist can strike in unexpected places. Since her early days, Nikki has become best known for her self-published yearly calendar that features her signature black-and-white color scheme of papercut art depicting imagery that illuminates her values, including hard work, patience, and nurturing those you love. In addition, she also produces her own posters, books, cards, and T-shirts. Nikki is a shining example of how to bring your values into your art and business, using her work to communicate the things she cares about—the power of love and hope, beauty in the everyday, care for the environment, and the potential to change the world for the better.

How did you begin making papercut art?

When I was in college, I worked in the ecology department, but I also enjoyed art; I thought that science drawings could bridge the two. I drew a lot of botanical and insect illustrations. As I was working to draw a fly exactly, I had an epiphany: nothing can be as perfect as the real fly itself. I questioned why I was trying to make perfect representations of things. A friend suggested I try cutting paper. It was very crude initially and everything was imperfect, but it freed me. It was all about reducing things to their essential forms.

How did your career as a self-employed artist begin?

Right around the time that I discovered that I loved making papercuts, I declared that I wanted to be an artist. One day, I decided to make a papercut book. I made the papercuts, had photostats taken at a printer (pre-scanner days), pasted the copies down onto paper, and then made copies at Kinko's. I used a lot of Wite-Out, white tape, and glue! I made two hundred copies and shopped them around to bookstores in Portland. From there I just kept making things on a small scale at first and put them out into the world.

How long does it take to make an illustration? What is your process like?

It really depends! Sometimes fifteen minutes, sometimes two months. Do I get to include the time I spend staring out the window, wandering on walks, sketching endlessly, and having meditative naps? My process starts with a walk in the morning. Then I come home and look through photos and make sketches. When I am ready, I transfer the sketches to black paper using graphite carbon paper. I then redraw over the carbon transfer and start cutting with an X-acto knife. I start by cutting the part that scares me the most. Once I get through the first cut, I don't fear mistakes as much.

How do you sell the originals? Do you keep some of them?

I usually have a show at the end of a series of work. I time it so that it coincides with the calendar or book publication month. I normally sell originals from my yearly calendar at Bryce's Barber Shop in Olympia, Washington, and at Land Gallery in Portland in October or November. They are also on sale at Buyolympia.com. Any remainders I sell through my site. I usually keep at least one piece from each series, which makes up the bulk of my traveling museum exhibit.

When you get an illustration commission, how do you go about charging the client for it?

I create a fee based on the days or hours that a project will take, and I make sure to cover the time that will be spent communicating and going over feedback, too. My decision to accept a job boils down to how much time it would take for me to make it, and if I'd rather use that time to spend with my family or doing personal work.

You are known for your books, journals, and also the popular calendar you put out each year. What do you enjoy most about making those products?

I found that I enjoy making things that encourage people to interact with each other in a positive way. I also like products used for personal introspection, like journals. The calendar includes mantras that may help people through difficult situations. The larger the audience for my work has become, the more I feel called to make work that is aligned with my values. I get stories from people all the time about how the calendar has carried them through despair to opportunity. The messages I use are kernels of hope that people can use to create change.

How do you go about self-publishing your calendar and some of your products?

In the beginning, I did everything myself, from printing and collating to binding. And then I found out there were machines that did all those things for you, so I started having the work done for me at local printshops. I produced only what I could fund and was capable of supporting. At first I produced 300, and the next year it was 750. Then I did 1,500, then 3,000. Each year it grew. (I produced 18,000 this year!)

FINDING YOUR VOICE

As an artist you have the opportunity to create your own unique stamp on the world. This is the artist's voice and it's a mixture of message, style, and technique. Everyone has a different process for finding his voice. It's not something you can simply learn through books or study. It requires you to pull from deep inside yourself to find what moves you and to express that through what you create.

Developing your voice can be a lifetime journey, a continual process of discovery and reinvention. As you get older, your values and drives may change and you may learn new techniques—and all this affects your voice and the work you create. Everyone's progress will be different, and there is always a bit of trial and error involved. If you create work that doesn't feel authentic, that's also an important realization—and helps eliminate what you shouldn't be doing.

Create Art for Yourself

Often when you start creating art, there's a common misunderstanding that there is one correct way to paint a picture or throw a pot—that the process you learned is the method everyone is supposed to use. Your initial technique will likely be a great foundation, but make sure it doesn't become so fixed that it locks you into just one style or even subject matter. It's an incredibly liberating moment to start making work that reflects your identity and core aesthetic—not that of your teachers or your classmates.

Take Risks

When making art, it can feel scary to change your work even slightly, especially if you are used to doing things in a particular way. But doing something differently, however small, automatically pushes your work to a new place. You can take small risks by using different colors than you normally use or adding or subtracting a medium. It might mean trying a new subject matter or narrative. In the process, you may discover that you need to take even larger risks. The results of these risks are what will set your work apart.

Push Through Difficulty

My painting teacher used to talk about the "painting curve," a line that looks like the letter U. He said that when you begin a painting (or other form of art), you are at the top of the U. Things look clean and wonderful in the beginning. But as you develop a piece of work, it often gets messier; that is the bottom of the painting curve. He insisted that working through the bottom of the painting curve—the point at which we think our work looks horrible or awkward—is critical to making good work. Working through the complexities of a piece to the point where it looks and feels wonderful again—rising back up to the top of the U—helps develop your technique as well as your unique voice.

Find What Inspires You

Inspiration does not always come to us in a flash. We often have to go in search of it, especially when we feel stuck. Finding inspiration means discovering the things that make you excited—even when they have nothing to do with your art practice. If you go on a trip, you might find inspiration in architecture, landscapes, or traditional patterns found in old cultures. Whatever speaks to you, infuse these visual stimuli from your life into your work.

To work through anxieties or find out what ignites your interest, it helps to carry a journal to do daily entries. Maintaining a journal with both written and visual thoughts is a long-standing tradition among artists that helps you ignite creativity and work through blocks. There is no right or wrong way to keep a journal. You can use a book with lined or unlined pages; it can be a written diary with stream-of-consciousness thoughts or a purely visual notebook with pages of drawings. One thing that is helpful, though, is to choose a journal size that is portable, so that you can carry it around with you. Make a habit of writing or drawing in your journal every day. Some days you'll have only a quick five minutes and other days a whole hour to devote to it. Don't worry about whether your writing makes sense or your ideas or drawings are any good. Eventually a pattern will emerge that will help unlock your mission as an artist and even identify new avenues for exploration.

Take a Break from the Internet

To home in on your voice, you must first abandon the messages in your mind that tell you how you *should* be doing something, so that you can free yourself to create art that is authentic to you. Sometimes we get caught in the trap of comparing ourselves to other artists. The Internet is a great place for artists to sell and promote their work, but it can also be a distraction. At any time, you can open your computer and have immediate access to the work of thousands upon thousands of artists. Looking at the work of other artists can be motivating, but it can also be intimidating. You might question whether your work is original enough or, conversely, whether you fit into any particular trend. Turning off the computer, finding your own inspiration, and exploring your own creative process may get you much further than studying the work of other visual artists.

Detach from Other Artists' Work

Many artists go through a period where they feel a need to make their work look like what they consider "good art," like creating work in a vein similar to their favorite contemporary artist or the work of an old master. Consciously or unconsciously, artists may initially hold ideas about what is acceptable and good and what is not. To carve out your artistic voice, you'll need to detach yourself from images of what you think constitutes successful work. This might mean a period where you avoid looking at the work of other artists on the Internet or books with images of your favorite work. "Pay attention to your inner compass," advises artist Josh Keyes. "It's easy to get caught up in the speed and blur of social media and exterior influences and expectations. Get to know your center and what propels and ignites your creativity."

LISA SOLOMON

Mixed media artist

OAKLAND, CALIFORNIA

WWW.LISASOLOMON.COM

Mixed media artist Lisa Solomon is prolific. She holds degrees from UC Berkeley (BA in Art Practice) and Mills College (MFA). Her work, reflecting an interest in hybridization specifically around domesticity and craft, has been featured in venues worldwide from the San Jose Museum of Art to the Koumi-Machi Kougen Museum in Japan. She has exhibited with various galleries including David Weinberg Photography in Chicago and Garson Baker Fine Art in New York and currently works with Walter Maciel Gallery in Los Angeles as well as Fouladi Projects in San Francisco. Her work has been featured in a monograph called *Hand/Made,* and she's also authored a book on embroidery titled *Knot Thread Stitch.* But despite leading a busy art practice, she also finds the time to blog and

teach art to students at San Francisco State University—using the lessons in her life to help guide the next generation of artists.

What role did your undergraduate experience have in where you are today?

I built a strong relationship with one of my art professors, Katherine Sherwood, at UC Berkeley. This was my first interaction with a working artist and it was extremely positive. She spoke about her work as a serious pursuit, not as a frivolous endeavor, and that changed the world for me. Learning from her made me realize I could become an artist, and it wouldn't matter if everyone else didn't take it as seriously as I did.

You worked at a gallery after you graduated from Berkeley. How did that job influence your career as an artist?

I first got a job waiting tables because I thought that if I worked nights, I would have my days to make art. But being outside school, I didn't end up using my days to make art even though I had set up a studio in my apartment. I decided to get a job in the field of art so I could find my place in it or at least get some inspiration and motivation. I found a job opening at Braunstein/Quay Gallery. So I called Katherine and another professor who had shown at that gallery. They put in a good word for me and I ended up getting the job. Not only did that job allow me to see how the art world works, I also saw exactly what a gallery does for an artist. I got to interact with working artists and saw that each artist had his own unique process and way of culling together an income. The experience motivated me to start painting and drawing again.

How much does discipline guide your own practice?

Being an artist requires a lot of focus and time. To get more disciplined, I came up with daily practices like drawing or photographing something every day and even posting the results on the Internet for accountability. Daily practices that take only fifteen minutes, such as a sketch or a small painting, force you to make something. You have to make art every day whether you feel like it or not in order to get somewhere, especially in the beginning of your career. Maybe you will find that you make your best work when you are bored or resistant!

How did you land your first gallery?

After I worked for Braunstein/Quay Gallery, I worked for Ed Russell at Graystone gallery in San Francisco before going to grad school. We remained close, and as I was finishing grad school I helped Ed with an art fair. He asked me to show some of my work alongside some of the artists he represented. And then, as if by luck, Richard Levy Gallery in New Mexico bought one of my pieces at the art fair and ended up taking me on as one of their artists. It was ironic because I'd told Ed that I didn't feel ready to show work at an art fair. I learned early on that it's important to do things that feel uncomfortable.

How did you get your monograph published?

It was the brainchild of MIEL, a publishing house located in Belgium. I "met" Éireann Lorsung, the owner, years ago through our blogs. We carried on an online friendship for many years. When I had an exhibition in Milan in 2011, Éireann offered to help me install my show. I was so grateful for her help and through that experience our friendship deepened. Later, she approached me to publish a monograph of my work—something I never imagined possible in my career.

How did you get your book deal for Knot Thread Stitch?

Knot Thread Stitch came about because an editor at Quarry knew of my blog and that I was into using embroidery in my art practice. She pitched the book to me. It happened when I was getting ready for my Milan exhibition. My daughter was two years old at the time. I also had returned to teaching. I didn't think I could fit in writing a book, too. I was scared beyond belief. But I started thinking this may be my only shot to make a book in my lifetime, so I took the plunge.

What advice do you give to your students on how to be successful once they are out of school?

First, it's important to deal with your fear and find a way to get over it. Fear is common among artists and it will paralyze you. And dealing with rejection is part of being in the art world. Allow yourself to wallow in the sadness that comes with rejection for a day, then dust yourself off and do it again. Continue to take risks, and over time you'll realize it becomes easier because you will also have some successes. Apply to juried shows and competitions. Make contact with a dream gallery. Create new work and ask a mentor for feedback. Come up with a studio schedule and stick to it. Last, be nice to others because the art world is small. Go to openings. Support your friends who are artists. Be a positive part of the art community. People may give you opportunities because your work is strong, but they are also likely to do so if you are kind, professional, and easy to work with.

FINDING TIME TO MAKE ART

If you're holding down a full-time job or raising a family, the thought of making time for art can feel like a luxury or an overwhelming addition to your schedule. You'll have to genuinely embrace the fact that your life might feel full for a while and that carving out time for art will require some discipline. Here are some simple ways that you can find time to make art:

.... *Schedule time.* Block out chunks of time in your calendar to make art, even if it's only two hours a week at first. Doing a little bit each week might not seem like a lot, but over time, it adds up.

.... *Incorporate art into your social activities.* Make art during quality time with your children, partner, or friends. Create collages with your kids on a Saturday afternoon or gather a group of friends to draw with you.

.... *Reduce screen time.* Use the time you normally spend surfing the Internet or watching television for making art instead.

.... *Delegate chores.* Having another family member take over a few chores can open up some free time for your art. If you're unable to pass any household duties to other people, don't feel bad about letting go of things.

.... *Bring a blank journal with you everywhere.* When pockets of time open up, you can pull it out to sketch, draw, or brainstorm ideas.

.... *Take an art class.* While it takes time, enrolling in classes will force you into art-making mode and onto a schedule. Going to a class can also lead to new creations, not to mention finessing your techniques or even adding a new one to your repertoire.

Setting up a space for your creative work is as vital as making time for your work. The important thing is to find space to dedicate to your creative process, even if it's a tiny corner of a room. First, make your space inviting. It helps to pin up pieces of inspiration, have a comfortable place to sit or stand, and keep the area clean and organized after every use. Also, you should have everything you need at your fingertips. Setting up an area that houses all of your supplies will free you up to create and eliminate potential excuses for why you cannot begin. Finally, make it your own, but be willing to make compromises. Sacrifices may be necessary, like moving your television to make room for an easel, and the space may also determine the scale of your art. For example, if you are a painter or sculptor, it may force you to work a bit smaller than you might like. If you need privacy when you work, make sure it's in a space in your home where you can place a room divider or close the door.

SURROUND YOURSELF WITH SUPPORT

When you are pursuing your dreams, you may encounter friends and family who tell you your goals are not possible. Surrounding yourself with people who support your aspirations and believe in your dreams will not only strengthen your confidence but also create connections that can further your career. Reach out to artists in your community who are also just kicking off their careers. If you admire someone's work or success, don't be afraid to ask them to coffee or invite them to see your work. Eventually, you will begin to build a community of friends. It's amazingly encouraging to get support from like-minded people, and you'll find you're also able to lend support to them. Many years later, those relationships will be some of the most important in your career.

2

GETTING DOWN *to* BUSINESS

Understanding how to run a small business is essential to making a living as an artist. The good news is that everyone possesses the ability to be a successful entrepreneur. With some basic tools, knowledge, and practice you can run your art business with dexterity. You may find that running an organized business brings you a tremendous amount of satisfaction and pride. In this chapter, we will cover the business basics: developing values and goals for your business, branding your business, exploring income streams, and setting up financial record-keeping—a big-picture-to-brass-tacks foundation that will set you firmly on the path to successful entrepreneurship.

EXPLORING DIFFERENT INCOME STREAMS

As you embark on your journey to become a professional artist, you'll need to determine the paths your art business will take. You'll have several options—like those presented in the following chapters, including selling original works and prints, illustration, and licensing. But where do you start? It may sound corny, but the best advice I got when I began my art career was "Follow your heart." There is no one blueprint that will work for everyone, so deciding what is best for you depends on the unique circumstances of your life, your strengths, your goals, your resources, and your experience.

Some artists are able to make a full-time living focusing mainly on one income stream, like illustration or fine art sales. But it's more common now to have multiple income streams. Diversifying your income is a great way to keep your artistic venture interesting and dynamic, and it also means that you won't be relying on one source of revenue. When one income stream becomes temporarily slow, another can pick up the slack. When you grow tired of a particular way of selling your work, you can focus on another for a while. Pursuing a passive income stream like licensing requires little or no additional work after the original image is sold, and yet you can earn royalty income over the course of years while you work to produce more original art.

As you go through the following chapters and assess each income stream, think about those you might enjoy the most and are the best fit for your work. Do not get caught up in choosing potential income sources because you think they sound the most profitable. If a source of income doesn't align with your values or sound enjoyable, it will eventually leave you feeling uninspired and inauthentic.

Starting small is the soundest approach, especially if you

> *It may sound corny, but the best advice I got when I began my art career was "Follow your heart."*

are still working at another job. Taking on too many income streams at once may cause you to feel overwhelmed. Devote your time to one or two streams and then, when you find your groove and begin earning, consider adding more. Perhaps you'll discover that managing an online shop takes up too much time or that dealing with illustration clients hampers your creative process. It's okay if an income source doesn't work out for you. Like finding your artistic voice, the process of exploring different ways of selling your work or earning from your talent requires a bit of trial and error and takes time. But with patience and an attitude of openness, you will eventually find your sweet spot.

KEEP YOUR DAY JOB, FOR NOW

It was true for many of the artists featured in this book, including me: we held on to our day jobs as long as we could until we were ready to strike out on our own. Day jobs may take up time, but they also provide financial security (which can support your transition into a career making art) and a solid routine. Over time, as your art business begins to grow, slowly try to transition out of your work schedule. It seems obvious to say, but when you work full-time at your day job, you have only evenings and weekends to make art. That can make sense when you're not yet making much money selling artwork or booking freelance jobs. But once you gain some market traction and bring in regular sales or gigs, you may want to consider going part-time at your job or finding part-time work. Eventually, you'll recognize you have enough—or close to enough—money coming in to work full-time on growing your art business. It feels like a leap of faith to leave a steady paycheck you have become accustomed to, but it is a leap that is worth taking!

ESTHER PEARL WATSON

Painter and illustrator

PASADENA, CALIFORNIA

WWW.ESTHERPEARLWATSON.COM

"I grew up poor in Texas. The one thing I was really good at was drawing. I knew from a young age that would be my ticket out of poverty," recalls Esther Pearl Watson. Indeed, her positive attitude has paid off. Since graduating from Art Center College of Design in 1993, where she met her husband, Mark Todd, they have become two of the country's best-known artists and illustrators. Shortly after graduating, they moved to New York to begin their careers and Esther entered strategic illustration competitions to make a name for herself. "Because the judges of *American Illustration* are the ones who hire illustrators, I was hired by publications like the *New Yorker*, *Rolling Stone*, *Details*," she notes. At the same time, Esther also pursued a fine art path. Her detail-rich, narrative paintings and drawings reflect her eccentric childhood and the characters that surrounded her. Esther's story is a testament to carving your own path and not waiting around for your career to take off.

You make your living from a variety of means: book and editorial illustrations, original painting sales, selling your own zines and comics, and teaching. What is it like for you to have such diversified income sources?

You are not bored, ever! It's important to remember that when you have diverse income sources, your main source of income often changes. In the beginning, illustration paid my bills, then painting sales. I am not a full-time teacher, so it provides a steady small paycheck for only a few months in the spring and fall. The great thing is that the ways you make your living bleed into each other a great deal. Everything I work on influences everything else. When I teach about color theory, I notice it influence my paintings. The personal fine art I make influences the illustration jobs that I get. But the flip side is that it's a lot of work! My husband Mark and I enjoy doing all the different aspects of our art practice ourselves, but sometimes this means sacrificing creative time. We have to be okay with distractions that take us out of the studio, especially since we have a child. It's a signal to us when our house gets really messy that we need to reorganize and slow down.

It's important to have boundaries about your work. Do you have criteria for what work you choose to do and what work you decline?

When you first start as an artist or illustrator, it's actually good to say yes to most of the work that comes your way—that's how you build connections and fill your portfolio. It's how you figure out what kind of work you like and don't like. Later, when you can be more discerning, you can choose companies and projects that you believe in.

We also feel it's important to get paid well for your work. When a company says, "You'll get great exposure, but we can't pay you," that can be a red flag! We do ask for more money for jobs if we are really busy. If nothing else, you should get paid for being busy!

In this age of online social networking, it's becoming less common for artists to practice in-person networking. Do you think it's still important?

There is nothing quite like making personal connections with people—potential clients, collectors, fellow artists. Selling your work to art directors or collectors is not just about the quality of your work—it's about personal connections. Every year, we try to go to the *American Illustration* party in November. Lots of people come out to that and you can meet a lot of new faces. We go to gallery shows. We are active on the Illustration Conference (ICON) board of directors, and we enjoy that conference for networking, too.

How do you balance being a good artist with being a good parent?

When you work at home, it can feel like you don't ever stop, as opposed to working in an office where you have set hours. And when you have a kid, it is especially important to separate work life from family life so your family gets priority. Sometimes it can feel difficult, or even crazy! Mark and I are extremely high-functioning in times of stress, but having a kid has forced us to have a more normal routine. No matter what we have going on in our work lives, we walk her to school, sit around the table for suppers, and have family outings.

You value your downtime, both with your family and by yourself. Why is relaxation important for working artists?

Mark and I have been doing this work for almost twenty years, and we can force ourselves to go beyond tiredness. But what happens is the quality of our work suffers. Downtime is creative time. You need that time to think about new ideas. Every day Mark and I walk Lili to school and then we walk around town and come home. It gives us time to talk to each other about what we have to accomplish that day and then we get home and get things done. We also exercise to manage stress. Daydreaming is also important time for artists. Simple things like eating well and sleeping do wonders. It's amazing how you can forget that when you are working so hard!

BUILDING YOUR VISION AND ACCOMPLISHING GOALS

One of the tools that will help you decide where to begin concentrating your efforts is goal-setting. First, you must create a vision for your future and take stock of your values to ensure that your goals are aligned with what is important to you. Then, putting together a goal-setting chart will help you actualize them. It's your personal tool—a guide toward meeting your goals. Start where you are now; you can always revise it later. Most of all, dream big and have fun!

Step 1: Build Your Vision Map

The first step in setting goals is to make a vision map for where you would like your art career to be in three to five years. These are your big over-arching goals and this is your opportunity to dream big, abandon doubt and fear, and use your imagination to think boldly about your future. Choose goals based on what sounds exciting to you now. Don't get tripped up with questions like "What if that's not realistic?" or "What if I end up not liking that?" It's common when you are mapping your future to question whether something is the right goal. At this stage, you don't need to worry about whether you'll enjoy it in the end. You can always revise your goals. Remember, you are the master of your future!

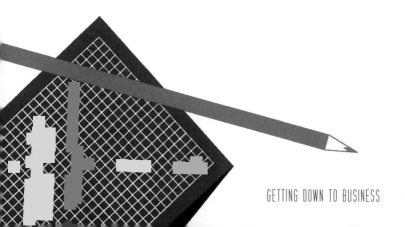

To make your vision map, write your name in the center of a sheet of paper and draw a circle around it. Then, write your vision statements on the lines reaching out from the center. It will look like an image of a sun with rays extending from it. Here are some examples of vision statements:

- Be represented by an illustration agency and get regular illustration jobs

- Spend my days making collages and get paid for it

- Have a lucrative online shop where I sell prints and original pieces

- Get my first solo show in a major gallery

- Illustrate a children's book

When you are finished making your map, pin it up in your work space or studio. Focusing on your vision of your future is a way of keeping yourself connected to the goals that are meaningful and exciting to you. Don't forget to revise it over time as other goals become more important to you or as you allow yourself to dream even bigger about your future.

Step 2: Articulate Your Values

Before you move on to setting intermediate goals based on your vision, it's important to know your values. One strategy for coming up with your list of values is to begin with the sentence "Selling my work will feel good as long as I . . ." or "I will feel good about my success as long as I . . ." Examples of values that might apply to you:

- If I take commercial work, I want to work only for companies whose products I would buy myself

- My work should get people to think differently

- Some of the work I create should be affordable

- When I create reproductions of my work, I will try to use materials that do not harm the environment

- I deserve to be paid well for my work

- People who buy my work should learn as much as possible about what they are purchasing

- A percentage of all my sales each year should go to charity

Articulating your values through your work and business will ensure that you execute your goals in a way that is most satisfying for you. You will not only feel good about the work you do, but you will also be able to make decisions with more purpose and clarity. For example, if you aim to license your work and one of your values is working only with companies whose products you would buy for yourself, then this value should help you make decisions about which clients you work with. Clarifying your values will also help you clearly communicate what your business is about to galleries, customers, collectors, suppliers, or potential clients.

Step 3: Set Intermediate Goals

To bring yourself closer to achieving the goals in your vision map, set intermediate goals that are small enough to accomplish over a few weeks to a couple of months. Think about the big goals from the vision map, and set one to three intermediate goals that will work toward achieving them. These intermediate goals should be concrete and actionable, so you can imagine what the results might look like once you meet them.

If one of your big goals is "Have a lucrative online shop where I sell prints and original pieces," then some of your intermediate goals might be:

- Set up an online shop to sell my work

- Find a high-quality printing lab to make prints of my work

- Come up with a name for my shop

- Photograph or scan all the original work I want to sell

Step 4: Develop Small Actionable Tasks

The final step in completing the chart is to develop short-term tasks to help you reach each intermediate goal on your chart. Get really detailed when you write short-term tasks. The smaller the task, the more likely you will complete it. Make sure each task is something you can complete in a few hours so that you have a sense of accomplishment each day.

If one of your intermediate goals is "Set up an online shop to sell prints of my work," examples of short-term tasks to reach this goal might be:

- Research online shop venues
- Talk to friends about online marketplaces they use to sell their work and learn the pros and cons of each
- Get paper and print samples from printing labs
- Determine what sizes of prints to sell in my shop
- Establish a pricing structure for my prints
- Determine what shipping supplies I need
- Purchase the shipping supplies
- Take photos of or scan my art to turn into prints
- Write descriptions of my prints
- Write my bio
- Design my logo or banner for my online shop

REBECCA REBOUCHÉ

Painter

NEW ORLEANS, LOUISIANA

WWW.REBECCAREBOUCHE.COM

Painter Rebecca Rebouché's upbringing was equal parts country and city: she grew up in the suburbs of New Orleans but spent summers in rural Louisiana. Rebecca lives a similar life now, splitting time between the bustling streets of New Orleans and the rural countryside of Franklin, Louisiana, where she has a retreat and studio. Rebecca's allegorical work is influenced by her connection to the Southern landscape, flora, and fauna, along with its tradition and lore. After attending school at Louisiana Tech University to study art and graphic design and stints in film and advertising, she came back to New Orleans to begin her journey as a working artist. By bringing her work to art festivals across the country, in just a few years she has amassed a loyal following of collectors. At her busy studio, she paints, draws, and manages a staff who help her promote, sell, package, and ship her work to customers across the globe. In addition to selling originals, prints, and other products in her online shop, she also licenses her work for home décor and gift products.

What steps did you take to become an artist and make it a full-time career?

I started a blog called Art for Breakfast where I would post a drawing each day. After a year, I had amassed a large collection of material. Then I decided I would do both my full-time job and pursue my art career for six months. This required ruthless "rules" and limitations. I gave myself a dress code: only jeans and black or white tops to cut down on time spent getting dressed in the morning, so that I would have time to journal. My parents made pots of gumbo and froze them in individual portions. After work, it was a system: defrost soup, eat, and go to the studio. Each week I chose ten drawings to turn into paintings. And each weekend I would set up at an art market in town to show the paintings. In the first week, I sold four paintings.

Then, something lucky happened: I got a jury summons and served for a month. I used that time in the courthouse "quiet room" to write a business plan. I also took a class at the Arts Council of New Orleans called Artist as Entrepreneur. With that class and my business plan, I quit my job the next month. Three months later I went on the road with only $100, to show at art festivals across the country. For the first show, I made a six-foot-tall painting of a red balloon that represented my hope and potential. I priced it high and thought it wouldn't sell but would serve as a centerpiece in my booth all summer. Instead, it sold at the very first show at full price! Suddenly I had money for gas and hotels. I didn't have a ton of paintings, so I would make art in hotel rooms between shows. I never went back to a full-time job again.

How do you manage your life outside the studio to make the most of your time in the studio?

When you are looking in from the outside, you think being a painter means you get to spend all day in a studio just painting, you'll have time to explore ideas, and it's easy to focus because you have total freedom and solitude. But that's simply not true. There is so much that must be done and only a small portion of it is painting. This means when you are painting, you need to be "on," making the most of that time. This requires three things: 1) You must care for your creative spirit so it is healthy; 2) You need to know what you don't have time for. For example, I pay someone to clean my house and studio. It's a small expense for the time it affords me; 3) You must batch your tasks. Honor important tasks like email and errands by giving them a place in your day or week. I prefer to handle email in the morning and I group all my errands together and do them on Fridays.

How does journaling inform your art practice?

Someone told me about the book *The Artist's Way*, which recommends writing three "morning pages" each day to get your thoughts and feelings on paper. I adopted this practice immediately. It gave me a new reason to get up in the morning. It kept me from feeling like my day was just a free fall into to-do lists, chores, and obligations. It allowed me a place to outline my dreams and make plans for the future. In my journal, my ideas are valuable and I can have everything I imagine. Usually I spend the first page complaining. It's a mental dumping ground. The second page is usually practical or just questions about big-picture goals such as "How will I ever write that book?" On the third page, I'm giving myself a pep talk. I let go of my limitations, outline practical steps, and give myself stepping-stones. I encourage my own vision and imagine the best-case scenario. Interestingly enough, I never set out to be creative. But even still, I get my best ideas in those pages. Journaling has become the most important element in my art practice and life.

What role does blogging play in your career and your success?

My blog connects me with customers and fans and allows them to feel like they know me. They feel invested in my success and sympathetic of my failures. It shows them that I'm a real person. The sale of art is only one step in an otherwise long process of gathering ideas, creating, sharing, and responding to the world. The blog gives real estate to all the other aspects of being an artist. Blogging creates a vast connection with something that is otherwise quite singular.

Where do you see yourself in the next three to five years?

I hope to publish a book that inspires and energizes others, establish my shop as an essential "piece" of New Orleans culture, have an exhibition in a new city, create larger and more expansive and expressive paintings, partner with a visionary brand/company that would expose my work to new and different people, and grow my circle of close contemporaries and artists I admire.

BRANDING YOUR BUSINESS

As an artist, you may assume that you don't need to think about the brand, or personality, of your business. Sure, the look and feel of your art helps establish the basis of your brand, but the personality of your business extends to many other aspects, from the design of your website to how you interact with buyers. Here are things to consider to effectively deliver your message:

.... *Integrate your core aesthetic into your brand.* Describe the core aesthetic of the work you make. For example, is it understated and minimal, vintage and nostalgic, or something else? Develop a logo, business card design, website, color scheme, and other graphics that communicate your aesthetic and complement your artwork. Some pieces, like your business card, can even include your art! If you maintain a consistent look by using the same typefaces, colors, or symbols, when people see your branding elements, they will know the work, site, or social media page belongs to you. If branding is not your strong suit, consider hiring a graphic designer to help you create a consistent look and feel.

.... *How you communicate and conduct business is a part of your brand.* For instance, consider how you share your core values through your website, social media presence, and email etiquette. When both your work and communication resonate with clients and customers, they will respect you and come back again.

SETTING UP THE NUTS AND BOLTS

Whether you plan to license your work, take illustration clients, sell paintings on the Internet, or set up a storefront, you are technically in business once you start receiving money for your art. You will be subject to laws and may need to get different licenses or permits, depending on where you are doing business.

Legal Structure

The most common legal structure for artists to operate under is a sole proprietorship (for solo artists) or a partnership (for one or more artists who band together on a joint business venture). For either, there is no paperwork that needs to be filed to set it up. Sole proprietors simply report their business income or loss on their personal income taxes every year. With partnerships, you report your income or loss depending on your share of the business. For instance, if you and a partner split the business fifty–fifty, then you would be responsible for paying taxes on 50 percent of the income or you could claim 50 percent of the loss. These legal structures work best for businesses that have low liability. If you are creating art that has increased liability—for example, large-scale sculptures or installations—you might want to file as an LLC, or limited liability company, which is a legal structure that does require paperwork. If you feel you are unsure about what structure to use, discuss with an accountant what legal structure would be best for you.

Business License and Zoning

Depending on where you live, you will most likely need to apply for a business license to legally run your business in your city (to find out, contact your city or county clerk). Business licenses often need to be renewed yearly and may require a flat fee or a fee based on your total business income for the previous year. Cities also have zoning requirements that delineate what types of work can be done in an area. For example, some places require people who want to run a business from their home to apply for a home occupation permit. In areas zoned for residential use, some cities may allow only home businesses that don't contribute to noise pollution or traffic. So if you are an artist who needs to operate loud machinery or you want to have a studio that customers can visit regularly, you may need to find a space outside of your home that allows this. Contact your local city government to learn more.

Seller's Permit

Many states require businesses to have a seller's permit if they plan to sell tangible goods to the public. Tangible goods are things you can touch, like paintings, sculptures, prints, and notecards. If your state imposes a sales tax, you'll be required to add tax to your customers' purchases. However, this does not apply to customers from other states who buy your goods online, though legislation may change on this. You will have to file a sales tax return periodically (ranging from monthly to yearly, depending on how much you sell in taxable goods) on the goods you've sold. The governing state agency that issues the permit is often the same entity where you will file the tax return. Also, if you plan to travel to another state to sell your goods, like at an art fair, you may also be required to file for a temporary seller's permit, collect taxes, and file a tax return on the sales you made with that state's agency. The good news is that having a seller's permit allows you to buy materials at wholesale prices or without sales tax from some suppliers.

Health Insurance

Typically, when you are self-employed, unless you are married or in a domestic partnership and your partner's employer extends benefits to you, you must purchase your own health insurance. Contact insurance companies in your area to find out the costs for individual insurance. If you were recently employed, your latest employer may offer a COBRA (Consolidated Omnibus Budget Reconciliation Act) plan, which extends the coverage you had at that job. Research artists or freelancers guilds and unions, like the Freelancers Union, which provide health care options for freelancers. You can also visit www.healthcare.gov to see what other low-cost health insurance plans are available to you.

Business Account

From the beginning it is important to manage your art as a business—and not a hobby—even if you are working elsewhere full- or part-time. You can start by opening a dedicated checking account for your business. If your business is operating under your name, you don't necessarily have to get a business bank account, though some banks' business accounts do offer special features for heavy account activity or if you have multiple employees, so it's worth looking into. If you decide to use credit cards, make sure you use a separate credit card strictly for your business. Having independent accounts for your business will help you keep all of your business income and expenses in one place, limiting any confusion with personal or family income and expenses.

Protect Your Work Through Copyright

The exposure the Internet offers artists can come with a downside: people can easily copy or reproduce your work without permission. Copyright laws protect your work, and understanding how they work is extremely important. In the United States, copyright is a form of protection for creators of "original works of authorship," including literary, dramatic, musical, artistic, and certain other intellectual works. Your work is copyrighted from the time your work is created in fixed, tangible form. In other words, the copyright immediately becomes your property once the art is created.

For an extra measure of protection, register your work with the U.S. Copyright Office. There are some benefits to doing this:

- You establish a public record of the copyright when you register it.

- If someone copies your work and you would like to file a lawsuit for infringement, that work must be registered.

- If you register your work, you can file it with U.S. Customs to protect against infringement in other countries.

Filing can happen at any time over the life of the work, so it's never too late to file any of your works. For more information about registering your works, go to www.copyright.gov. Outside the United States, check your government website for more information on copyright. If you believe your copyright has been infringed, contact a lawyer for a consultation.

MANAGING YOUR ARTIST INCOME

The most distinct difference you'll notice between an artist's income and the income you earn at a job is that you won't get a regular paycheck. When you do get paid it's in the form of sales from customers or payments from clients, and no tax has been withheld. While you can make a healthy income over the course of a year, your earnings will likely come in inconsistent intervals.

Since your income will arrive sporadically, it's a good habit to save money. Deposit money set aside for taxes or a rainy day into a savings account specifically for your business. That way, every time you get a big check from a client or sell a painting, for instance, you can put a portion of the check into this account. This account can cover tax payments or unexpected business expenses, like a deposit on a new studio space. It's also reassuring to know that there is a pool of money set aside in case you go through a period when clients are slow in paying or your art sales are less frequent.

> *While you can make a healthy income over the course of a year, your earnings will likely come in inconsistent intervals.*

Tracking Income and Expenses

It's beneficial to document your income and expenses through spreadsheets or bookkeeping software as early and regularly as possible to begin cultivating good habits. Knowing at all times how much money is coming in and out of your business and from what sources gives you information that can instruct many of your decisions. For example, you may discover that you incur most of your business expenses during the beginning of the year but most of your income comes during the summer months. This information can help you to understand your cash flow and make appropriate savings plans. Also, your expenses—things that you accumulate expressly for your business, like a computer, paintbrushes, and camera lenses—may be considered tax deductible, so it's good to maintain a record of them. Keep receipts for business expenses that you pay for with cash, or pay for them using your business bank card. And if your business is conducted in a room in your home dedicated to your business only, some percentage of your living expenses like your rent or mortgage and utilities may be deductible. A detailed exploration of tax laws and other helpful resources are available through the IRS small business and self-employed tax center website (www.irs.gov).

You might start out simply using Excel spreadsheets to track your expenses. Eventually, most freelance artists graduate to using accounting software such as QuickBooks or Sage (formerly Peachtree) or online services such as FreshBooks or Kashoo, to keep their books (see Resources for more information). You might also consider working with an accountant who uses the reports you generate to determine your yearly taxes. Many of these programs also help you create invoices and sales receipts, generate profit and loss and sales tax liability reports, and track your inventory. If you are not comfortable with maintaining your books, consider hiring a bookkeeper or accountant to help you set up a system or manage this part of your business. Be realistic about your natural strengths and weaknesses; if tracking your income is nothing but stressful, then it's probably a good idea to outsource that while you direct your energy toward the aspects of managing your business that come more naturally to you.

Filing Taxes

When you maintain your books regularly, you'll see what your yearly income is shaping up to be. Knowing how much you are earning and spending also keeps you from going too far into the red, though it is normal to have some income loss in the first year or two of business. In the United States, it's recommended that self-employed workers, like artists, pay quarterly taxes based on their projected income for that year. Your estimated tax is often based on your income from the previous year, but you can make adjustments to more accurately reflect your current income. It's important to set aside about 20 to 40 percent of your total income each month in a savings account to anticipate paying any taxes (you can talk to your accountant to get a percentage that's appropriate for you).

ORGANIZING YOUR TIME

Being your own boss comes with a lot of freedom, and that is a good thing, because you get to decide how you will spend your day. It's also one of the most challenging aspects of your new life as an entrepreneur! If you are used to being on a schedule—whether it's at school or a job—knowing how to best organize your day and set regular work hours can be tough at first.

Setting up a schedule to organize your day will help you accomplish your daily goals. Your art business will come with responsibilities, like managing an online shop, bookkeeping, packing, shipping, and email correspondence. As you develop a work schedule that works for you based on your preferences and work style, here are some things to consider:

.... *Assign yourself consistent work hours and breaks.* Are you someone who likes to work "regular" hours like a nine-to-five gig? Or do you prefer to start earlier and end your workday much later, but punctuate it with plenty of breaks? Breaking up your day to do a little exercise and get nourishment will keep you energized to do your best work. Experiment to determine what is the most productive schedule for you, then assign yourself set hours—and stick to them.

.... *Divide your day into different genres of tasks.* Creating a schedule that breaks your day into manageable chunks of time dedicated to specific activities lends a sense of order and ensures that you are attending to all your varied responsibilities. For example, if you feel most creative later in the day, set aside the first hour of your day to answer emails, make phone calls, and organize your calendar. You can use the rest of the morning to take care of administrative things like research, printing reference material, bookkeeping, and sending work to clients. Then, your afternoons or evenings are when you make your art.

.... *Create a list daily.* Make a list of what you need to accomplish each day and prioritize items. Your list can be digital or hand-written—whatever works for you. You might find making a list on your phone or computer is more flexible because you can shift what you will do each day during the week as your priorities change without having to rewrite or reorder your list again and again. When you have a list, you can focus on taking action. Conversely, if you keep too many priorities in your head, you may lose track of what you need to do. Make your to-do list your best friend!

ORGANIZING YOUR FILES

One of the most exciting parts about being an artist is watching your body of work grow. And the more prolific you become, the more work you'll need to store, both physically and digitally. Even if you work only by hand, scanning or photographing your work at a high resolution and storing it for easy access is critical for efficient communication and sales. If a magazine editor emails and says, "We'd like to feature one of your paintings in our next issue and we need a high-resolution image today," you should be ready to send off the file in no time. And as a working artist, you can continue to make money off of artwork even years after you've sold the original, through things like licensing or print sales. A lifetime of digital files will someday become the most valuable thing you own!

Organizing Originals

Taking care of your original work and storing it appropriately is essential to protect your art from damage and to ensure that it will be in pristine condition when you deliver it to a buyer. The first rule of thumb is to store all of your artwork in a cool, dry place. The effects of light, heat, and moisture can destroy artwork in a very short period of time. Wrap your works securely to protect them from sunlight, scratches, dust, or other potential damage. Cellophane sleeves can be great protectors for smaller works on paper. For large sculptures or paintings, you may need some bubble wrap or foam. Find a space to store the works and make sure that they are properly labeled on the outside of the protective packaging so that you can easily locate them when you need them. If your art is small or rendered on paper, flat files are a great way to store work. Purchasing a new flat file cabinet can be expensive, but it is often possible to find used flat files at estate sales or on a site like Craigslist for much less. If flat files are not available, you can store the pieces in filing cabinets or boxes.

Organizing Digital Files

Maintaining organized digital files is just as important as physically storing and organizing original work. Once a work is finished, scan or photograph it, even if it is personal work that you have no intention of selling. Keeping a record of all of your work and then organizing the records on your computer will save you time in the future—especially when press calls, you need an image for an exhibition catalog, or you want to enter a competition on a deadline. In addition to keeping files organized on your own computer, you should also back up your files on a cloud system or external hard drive.

When developing your digital system, first create a set of master folders with overarching categories. Select categories that make the most sense for you.

> *Once a work is finished, scan or photograph it, even if it's personal work that you have no intention of selling.*

For example, how do you think about your work? Do you list them in a certain way on your website? You might organize files on your computer by master categories such as medium or project type. And then you can further organize within each master category. What's important is that you create a system that's intuitive and works for you.

Once you have set up your folder system, the next step is to name your files. Again, the important thing is that your file-naming system makes sense for you, since you are the person who will need to find the images once they've been filed. Consistency is what matters most, so use a file-naming convention with a set of consistent identifiers. A good file-naming convention makes it easy to find your work. You could begin your file-naming convention with the name of the master folder, followed by the name of the piece and whether the image is high- or low-resolution. Never simply use the name of the piece to identify it! If you make a lot of work, you may forget what you named a piece, and that's where you may run into trouble when trying to locate digital files. Some people like to add dates, client names, or project names to their file-naming conventions, too.

Your file naming system may look like this:

type of art_name of piece_date_resolution

examples:
painting_Sunrise_Oct2015_hires
drawing_HorseIV_Jan2016_lowres

Or, maybe it looks like this:

client_ name of piece_ date_resolution

examples:
NYTimes_BeijingCityGuide_5.2014_hires
OscarHaynes_BirthAnnouncement_1.2014_hires

PROMOTING *your* WORK

Once you've built a body of work and are ready to begin getting it into the hands of customers, your job is to promote, promote, promote! Marketing may feel daunting (and even foreign if you've never done it before), but promoting your work can be just as creative and fulfilling as making your artwork. There has also never been a better time to get your work out into the world in a more cost-effective and engaging way. Social media platforms like Facebook, Twitter, Pinterest, and Instagram are all effective (and mostly free) ways to publicize your work. In addition, designing a strong web identity, blogging, creating eye-catching postcards, and even talking about your work to strangers can yield great results. And you don't have to do it all yourself, either. Magazines and blogs are looking to feature the work of artists, and all it takes is a little savvy to get them to notice you. By the end of this chapter, you'll have the tools to develop a strategic marketing plan to get your art business off the ground.

CREATING A STRONG WEBSITE

The Internet has become *the* place for artists to share and plug their work. Creating a website that showcases your work is an important way to establish yourself as an artist. Your website is often one of the first places that people—customers, gallery owners, collectors, art directors—will encounter the breadth of your art and brand. Since first impressions are everything, investing resources in creating a site to show and sell your work will go a long way. And there are many ways to create a clean, easy-to-navigate, professional-looking website, even on a limited budget. Site hosts like Virb, WordPress, and Cargo Collective, among others, offer free or low-cost templates or themes that you can customize. You can also barter your art with a designer to produce your website for you!

In terms of design, it can be overwhelming to make decisions; building a website is often one of the tasks we put off the longest. Spend an hour or two perusing other artists' sites and take note of the ones you spend the most time on. What keeps you there? What are intuitive ways to browse through work? Are there fonts or color palettes that would best showcase your pieces? You never want to rip another artist off, but observing what you do and don't like will arm you with vital information about how you want to build your own site.

Here are some important components to an artist's website:

.... *Function.* Make sure your website is easy to navigate. Ask people you know to test your site on multiple browsers and give you feedback about how easy it is to find what they need.

.... *Clean design.* Remember, you want to highlight your artwork! A simple background and overall design that doesn't compete for attention with your art will guarantee that your art gets top billing on your site.

.... *Clear domain name.* When selecting a domain name, make sure it's clear and easy to remember—and aligned with the rest of your online presence and branding. Most artists simply use their first and last name as their domain name (e.g., johnnyjones.com), but that's not necessary if it's already taken or your company has another name. The important thing is that it's simple and memorable.

.... *Strategic selection of work.* As you grow as an artist, your body of work will expand in size and scope. You will need to select your best or most relevant work to highlight. Don't show everything you've ever made! If you work in a number of different styles or media, organize your work in a way that's easy for website visitors to find what they need. For example, you might divide your work into categories that reflect the subject matter and then choose the best examples in each category to show on your website. Or, sometimes artists divide their portfolios by medium or by the year it was created. Do what makes the most sense for you and how you think people will want to browse your work.

.... *Bio.* You are not just selling your art; you are selling yourself as the artist. Let people know who you are as a person. Share your interests and what inspires you. Include a photograph of yourself and tell people in what city or area you live. If you are seeking illustration work, you can include a list of clients on this page, too.

.... *Press.* Some artists include a press page on their website. It's not necessary, but if you have gotten press that you are proud of, your website is a great place to display to it. Press lends cachet to your brand! If you have it, flaunt it.

.... *Contact information.* People interested in working with you or buying your work need to know how to get in touch. Make your contact information clear, including an email address and any links to social media or your blog, so they can follow you there. You may also include a link to sign up for your newsletter/ mailing list.

.... *Shop.* Never make people hunt for how to buy your work! If you have an online shop, your website is a place to link to it. Your site may have a shop embedded, or you might have an external shop like Etsy or Big Cartel. If there are multiple ways for people to buy your work, you might consider a store locator page to direct customers to retailers who carry your original works or products.

WRITING A BIO

As artists, we might like to believe our work speaks for and sells itself—and that would be enough. While your work can speak volumes, a well-crafted bio that you can use on your website or for press outreach can help develop a fuller picture of who you are as an artist, including your background, motivations, and accomplishments. The more written information there is about you and your work on your website, the greater the chances that bloggers and print media will find reasons to write about you and share your work. Here are some important things to remember when crafting your bio:

.... *Keep it simple.* Your bio should be one or two paragraphs so people don't feel overwhelmed with text. You can keep a more thorough bio on hand (or link to one on a separate page of your website or blog) for those who might be interested.

.... *Use a consistent and active voice.* Write in either the first ("I am a mixed media artist based in Chicago") or third ("Jane Jones is a mixed media artist based in Chicago") person, but make sure you are consistent throughout. Use an active voice; it's more dynamic.

.... *Share interesting things about yourself to engage your audience.* Let people get to know you: Where did you grow up? Do you have a family? Do any of these things influence your work? What do you enjoy doing outside of making art?

.... *Write about some of your accomplishments.* Have you won awards or been included in juried shows? People who are thinking about buying your work or hiring you for illustration might want to know these things! Don't be shy about your achievements.

KEEPING A BLOG

If you are looking to establish a relationship with fans and customers, blogging is a great way to go. A blog is a dynamic platform to share your talents, inspirations, and accomplishments. Unlike a static website, the point of a blog is for you to add new content every day, or as often as you like to post. Keeping a blog offers an opportunity for your audience to learn more about you and your work over time and provides a forum for them to interact with you. You can let readers leave comments and you can respond to them, creating a dialogue. Many blogs also make it easy for readers to share your posts on Facebook and Twitter or images from your posts on Pinterest, allowing the audience for your blog to expand on a daily basis.

Setting up a blog is easy. Many blog platforms like Typepad, Word-Press, and Blogger offer free or low-cost, easy-to-use templates. If you want a more unique blog, it is possible to hire a web designer (or the same person who designed your website) to create a blog for you with compatible design elements. Either way, make sure you design your blog—the banner, fonts, and sidebar elements—in a style that's in line with your brand, as discussed in chapter 2.

Blogging doesn't have to be time-consuming, either. Tumblr, a short-form blog format for posting visual media, is a great option for artists who don't have time to prepare lengthier written posts. And taking blogging breaks is totally normal, too. Even professional bloggers occasionally alter their schedule to give themselves a break or a vacation. Just make sure to announce your breaks to your readers. They will appreciate knowing this in advance and feel comforted that you'll be back.

In addition to posting new work or promoting a show or opening, your blog can also be a place to offer a behind-the-scenes look at your creative process and share pictures from relevant art events. Sharing your journey as an artist on your blog can make you feel more confident about your work, inspire others to take risks themselves, and, of course, generate new interest in your work.

Blogging isn't for everyone, however. I recommend starting a blog and keeping a regular schedule for one or two months to find out if it's something you enjoy. It's worth experimenting with, but you may learn in the process that it doesn't fit your personality or work style. Your blog should be something you look forward to keeping, so finding your particular groove is important. Here are some tips for keeping a regular blog:

.... *Decide on a realistic posting frequency.* Some artists post on their blog daily. For others, once or twice a week is more their speed. Whatever you decide, remain consistent so that your readers know what to expect. Note your frequency on your "About" page, so that it holds you accountable to your posting schedule. And remember, it's okay to take a break every now and again!

.... *Prepare easy solutions for those days when you don't have more lengthy content.* Not every blog post has to be in-depth or image heavy! You can post a couple of images from a favorite artist or the scan of a quick sketch you made over the weekend. In fact, mixing quick and easy posts with more in-depth entries will give your readers some variety.

.... *Choose a format that works for you.* Maybe all your posts are images without much text. Or maybe you like creating long posts that go up once a week. There is no right or wrong way to do it, so create a format that fits your lifestyle and writing habits.

.... *Post about things that you enjoy and blog for yourself above all else.* If you create blog content simply because you think it's what people want to see or hear, you will lose interest in blogging quickly. Keep the focus on what you love or are intrigued by, and your enthusiasm will be contagious.

Writing a Good Blog Post

Blogging is most successful when you are yourself—both in your approach to blogging and in the type of posts you write. The first rule of thumb is to write about things that you are genuinely interested in and that inspire you. You also want to write in a way that comes naturally to you. Use your own voice and talk to your readers as you would if they were sitting next to you at a café. Don't worry too much about the length of your posts. When I first started blogging, my posts were pretty short—just one image and a short paragraph. I hadn't yet figured out what I was comfortable revealing about my work and my life. Over the course of time, I became more comfortable sharing more of my work, my process, and parts of my life with my readers. Go with your gut: if you feel that you have revealed too much, then you probably have. Use your own sense of propriety to gauge what you want to talk about and at what length.

Let's not forget about images! As an artist, you are likely attracting readers who enjoy visual stimulation, so include strong imagery. Even when I am writing about a topic that may have little to do with my art, I still post an engaging photograph or an image of my work that relates to the post's topic. And remember, if the image you post doesn't belong to you, always give the artist or photographer credit. It's always great to email the artist to ask how they'd like their work to be credited. Most artists or photographers simply want their name included next to the image and a link to their website or blog. Others may have more specific requests.

USING SOCIAL MEDIA TO PROMOTE YOUR ART

A virtual form of word of mouth, social media allows you to share your work and make connections in ways that might have been unimaginable just a few years ago. In my own career, I credit social media with getting my work in front of a wide audience and, as a result, my being able to make a living from it. Through slowly growing my social media presence over the past several years, I have made connections with hundreds of new customers and gotten exposure for new illustration work and commissions.

Your social media network can become a significant part of your customer base. Social networking platforms that are helpful for artists are Facebook, Twitter, Pinterest, and Instagram. Best of all, they are free and easy to use. If you are new to social media, begin with just one or two platforms. Familiarize yourself with them and gauge whether they're something you might be able to manage and update with some frequency. Don't spread yourself thinly across many platforms, or you might find yourself juggling too much. If you decide to use several platforms, it's best to be consistent and choose the same user name for all—one that is short, easy to remember, and makes sense—like using your name or business name.

And while social media is a great marketing tool, it can also serve as a distraction from creating actual work! You may even find yourself feeling like a teenager again, since social media can sometimes feel like a popularity contest. There will always be another artist who has more followers or fans. So if you find yourself feeling jealous, getting caught up in monitoring your statistics, or feeling disappointed when no one has commented on your Facebook post, remember that it takes time to gain fans. The more people see your name over and over in different parts of the Internet, the more people will recognize you and your work—which will lead to more interactions. Look at social media as an opportunity to build a supportive community with your peers, not compete with them.

Facebook

It's hard to remember a time when we didn't connect with people using Facebook. Facebook fan pages are an effective way to share what you're up to with people who enjoy your work. If you haven't already, create a business fan page that is separate from your personal page. Unlike your personal page, your fan page is public and anyone can follow. Posts on your fan page can direct people to your website or blog and create another way for fans to interact with you. You can invite friends to your fan page, and many of these people can share your page with their friends, resulting in exponential growth.

If you don't know what to post on your fan page, an easy solution is to make your fan page a gateway to your other Internet content. For example, you can use your Facebook fan page daily during the week to link to your blog posts as well as images of your work on your website, products in your Etsy shop, press you've received on blogs, or glimpses of what you're working on. "Giving sneak peeks of a work in progress on your Facebook page is a lot like a theatrical movie trailer," notes artist Josh Keyes. "It keeps folks wondering how it will develop and what it will look like when it's done." You can also share invitations to events like art openings. Once a follower sees your post in their feed, they can comment on it and ask you questions, or share the link with their friends.

Twitter

You've probably heard of Twitter, but you might not be sure how to use it to promote your work. Twitter is a social networking service where you can post messages of up to 140 characters, known as "tweets." Each user picks a user name, called a handle, that begins with the @ symbol. You will also have a Twitter avatar—a small thumbnail photo, which can be your logo, artwork, or your portrait.

Since you'll be using Twitter for your business, it's best to have a public (and not private) account. If you are a private person, you can use your

Twitter account strictly for business purposes to promote your artwork, share recent press, as well as share links to things you find interesting online. You don't have to reveal the details of your personal life! You get to decide what you post. At a minimum, tweet out all the content that appears on your blog and other relevant news about your art or events. Interact with and give praise to other artists you admire. Following and tweeting about fellow artists and entrepreneurs helps build community. For example, if you are interested in illustration, find illustration-focused bloggers or organizations to follow on Twitter. If you are interested in showing with galleries, follow galleries that interest you. When you follow people and interact with them, it increases the chances that they will follow you back and may even lead to more conversations through tweeting. If you are new to Twitter, you'll want to learn the following terms:

@username: This is a Twitter handle, the name you use on your Twitter account. Whenever someone includes your handle in a tweet, it will appear in your mentions feed.

Retweet: When you come across a tweet in your feed that you'd like to share verbatim with your followers and without any commentary, you can "retweet" it using the retweet link, usually found below every tweet.

RT: This is an abbreviation for retweet, but it's used when you want to retweet something and also comment on it within the same tweet. It's a great way to interact with someone and share a tweet at the same time. For example, if @lisacongdon tweets "So excited about the release of Art Inc with @chroniclebooks," you can place a comment at the beginning of the retweet that says: "Can't wait! RT @lisacongdon So excited about the release of Art Inc with @chroniclebooks."

 # (hashtag): Tweets can be categorized if you use hashtags, or the # symbol in front of any word or set of words strung together without spaces (for instance, #artfair). When someone clicks on the hashtag, they will see all the tweets that used that same hashtag. If you're at a big event or conference, they often provide you with a hashtag to use, and it's an easy way to see what others are saying about the event.

Messages: You can send short private messages to others on Twitter who follow you, depending on how they have their preferences set.

Shortened URLs: Because of the 140-character limit, Twitter will often abbreviate any URL you place in your tweet. But if you need to cut it further, to accommodate more room for your own words, you can use URL-shortening sites like Bit.ly and TinyURL. At those sites, you can enter any URL and it will spit out a shorter URL to use in your tweet.

Pinterest

As an artist, you are probably a collector of visual imagery, and Pinterest can aid in this effort. Pinterest is a photo-sharing website that allows users to curate their own "pinboards," or page of images they choose organized around a theme. Many artists use this visually rich social platform to collect inspiration and share their work. Users can browse the pinboards of other users, "re-pin" images to their own pinboards, or "like" photos. To get started on Pinterest, first set up a profile that includes keywords to describe your interests and your website address (so followers can find you outside the platform).

Before you pin images of your art, it's often a good idea to add a small signature or logo on the bottom to protect it, as it's very easy for people to take or share images from Pinterest without giving credit or linking to the original source. When you pin a photo of your work, include a short description as well. Pinterest is searchable, so keywords are a great way to help people find your pins. For instance, if I pin one of my paintings of a forest of birch trees, I'd use keywords such as "birch," "trees," "forest," and "nature" in my description. This might sound simple, but the more descriptive your keywords, the more likely it is that others will find your work. Finally, be sure to attach a link that points back to your website or blog. You can also get more exposure for your work and even generate sales by including the price for the item in your description. This simple trick will add your pin to the "Gifts" section on Pinterest and will display the price on the front of the image throughout the site.

Instagram

The visual arts and Instagram are a match made in heaven. Instagram is an online photo-sharing and social networking app used primarily on mobile devices. Users take pictures with their smartphone or mobile device, apply digital filters to them, and share them with followers. You can "like" and comment on the images of other users. The app allows you to share the image on other portals like Facebook and Twitter, and it also publishes your images on the Instagram website. Like on Twitter, user names, or handles, begin with the @ symbol. Use the same handle as you do on Twitter to keep things seamless. Every day, artists use Instagram to take their followers behind the scenes, to share their studio spaces, processes, and new work, as well as to promote shows and other accomplishments. I've even gotten several commission requests from Instagram followers and have sold pieces of art simply by posting images of my studio, so it also has the potential to become a sales tool!

SOCIAL MEDIA BASICS

While these social media platforms are easy to use, knowing how to use them well will help you grow a dedicated following. Here are some recommendations for making the most out of your social media pursuits:

.... *Start small.* Begin with one or two platforms, like Twitter and Facebook, to establish your social media presence and post as frequently as you can. Work on building community by commenting on both platforms, sharing other users' posts in Facebook, and retweeting other users' posts in Twitter. Though it might take time, eventually social media karma will set in, and people will start to return the favor and follow you. Once you feel like you've gotten a foothold in either platform, you can consider trying another one.

.... *Be responsive.* When followers show an interest in your work and ask questions or make comments, show them you care and respond to their queries or compliments. This engages people with what you do and establishes a level of goodwill, making them more inclined to maintain contact with you, purchase your work, or hire you for a commission.

- *Stay positive.* Keep the tone of your Facebook and Twitter feeds upbeat and engaging and avoid, at all costs, negative posts or comments. It can be tempting when you are having a bad day to share your frustrations on your Facebook fan page or Twitter feed, but negative posts can turn followers off.

- *Share some of yourself.* Collectors usually make buying decisions based on more than just the work of art—they want to know and like the artist, too. Social media tools can give potential buyers or clients frequent glimpses into your personality and interests.

- *Market, market, market.* When you complete new works and add them to your website, don't miss any opportunity to promote them by posting on your Facebook fan page, tweeting links to them, adding them to your Pinterest board, and sharing photographs of them on Instagram. You never know who may be following you!

- *Celebrate your successes.* It helps build your credibility when you announce accomplishments like awards, commissions, and media coverage right when they happen. You might be uncomfortable with the idea of tooting your own horn, but sharing your achievements will help you establish yourself in the art market.

- *Keep a balance.* While social media is a great place to talk about your work and make announcements about press or sales, it can be a turnoff for followers if they constantly hear too many marketing-type posts from you. Pay attention to the type of posts you make and their frequency. At most, limit marketing-type posts to no more than two times a day on Twitter and once a day on your Facebook fan page, and make sure they are surrounded by plenty of nonmarketing posts.

XXXXXXXXXXXXXXXX

CLAIRE DESJARDINS

Painter

MONTREAL, CANADA

WWW.CLAIREDESJARDINS.COM

Montreal native Claire Desjardins spent her childhood summers in the countryside, where she discovered painting. But although she loved the art form, she chose to study business in college as a way to a stable, well-paying career. After graduating, she worked for ten years in technology and marketing. Several years ago, she set up a painting studio at home to get back in touch with her creative side, painting for the first time since she was a child. Over time, she moved from small to large canvases and began painting abstractly. By 2011, she was selling enough of her work to pursue art full-time. Since then, Claire has received grants to attend artist residencies at the Vermont Studio Center and Da Wang Culture Highland in Southeastern China. She is represented by Galerie Lydia

Monaro in Montreal and Muse Gallery in Toronto and is a top-selling artist on Saatchi Online. Claire's work can be found in both private and corporate collections around the world.

As a self-taught abstract painter, how did you go from painting in your studio to selling work?

I'd been painting for several years, and around the advent of Facebook, I started posting my work there. I had given a painting to a friend and then another friend of his saw it on Facebook and he contacted me about whether I had anything else for sale. That was how it all started. I began meeting a lot of people online who were interested in my art. That year I did quite well with my art, but I was still working for a marketing communications company. I worked only four days a week, so I would paint on my free weekday. My company was restructuring and merging, and I got laid off in 2011. But it was a perfect time for me to leave my job.

How did you first get gallery representation?

I sold a painting to one of my fans on Facebook. It was one of my first paintings that I had sold to someone I didn't even know, so it was pretty exciting. I made sure that I really took care of her. I packed the painting properly, sent it with a booklet of my art, and called her to make sure everything went smoothly. Sometime later, I received an email from Muse Gallery in Toronto. Apparently, the woman from Facebook who bought my painting lived around the corner from the gallery and had told them about me. The gallery owner looked me up, liked what he saw, and contacted me to work on an artist agreement together. I did some research on them and called other artists who the gallery represented. I asked them about their relationships with the gallery and eventually, it all came together. I borrowed my father's minivan and drove a bunch of paintings to Toronto! They have represented me since and have given me a couple of solo shows, too.

Right around the time you left your job, Anthropologie contacted you. They sell your original paintings and license your paintings to make prints and for use on their products. How did this relationship come about? What are the advantages and disadvantages of working with a big company to sell and license your work?

It all began one day when I got an email—and in the subject line it said "Anthropologie Interest." They were looking for local artists to feature on the walls and windows of the new Montreal store. Four of their buyers came to my studio. I heard that they had read about me on Mocoloco.com.

There are both advantages and disadvantages to working with a large company. The main and obvious advantage is the exposure of my art. Other advantages include the additional revenue, as well as seeing my art on different products. The disadvantage is less obvious; it's that a small portion of the artistic community came to perceive my art as too commercial or that I'm "selling out."

What is your main mode for selling original work now?

By far, I make most of my sales online. Specifically, I've had success with Saatchi Online. In order to nurture this relationship, I try to keep up with my social networking as much as possible. This is a very important component to my job, as it's the only advertising I can afford (it's mostly free!), and it reaches so many people. Whenever I post a new painting online, I make sure to link it to a page that allows people to purchase my art, like Saatchi Online. I make sure that I give them credit for the good things that they do, in a timely fashion. So if they include one of my pieces on their home page, I make sure that I blurt it out for all to read, on all my social media like Facebook, LinkedIn, Pinterest, and Twitter.

You are an advocate for signed agreements—whether in licensing or when you work with galleries. Why are they important?

When you sell or license your art, money and image rights are involved, so spelling out the rules in advance helps to manage expectations and eliminate surprises later on. It protects both the artist and the reseller. Proposing the writing of an agreement should not be perceived as an unfriendly gesture or an indication of mistrust. In fact, it should be considered an act of ensuring mutual understanding. We all have contracts with our cable or cell phone companies, so why wouldn't you have an agreement with the resellers of your art, whether they are galleries, agents, or commercial companies? The exercise of writing an agreement will raise many questions that had not been thought about before. Those questions can be imperative in terms of the health and sustainability of the relationship.

NEWSLETTERS AND EMAIL BLASTS

With so many social media options, it may feel redundant to send an email newsletter or blast to make announcements, but they are still a viable and effective way to maintain contact with fans of your work, especially those who may not be active on social media. They are a great way to promote shows, inform fans of a sale happening in your shop, or let people know you are participating in an upcoming art or craft fair. To build your mailing list, you'll need to provide a way for people to sign up on your website. You can also collect emails in person when you participate in art or craft fairs or teach classes by providing a sign-up list. It's important to add people to your list only if they have asked to be added.

The next step is to choose an email marketing service (see Resources). Many provide templates and organizational tools, and send your email blast or newsletter. You can insert your own graphics and images into the templates, or if you are familiar with HTML, you can make them more personalized and unique. Most services will also track the data associated with each mailing, including how many people opened your mail, clicked on links, and unsubscribed from future mailings, as well as how many emails bounced. When you begin sending emails, remember to limit the amount of blasts you send out—monthly or quarterly is sufficient. Otherwise, people may consider them a nuisance and unsubscribe.

PRINT PROMOTIONAL MATERIALS

In this digital age, we may be inclined to forget the power of print. Yet, there still is nothing like a tangible postcard or business card to help spread the word about your work, upcoming shows, or studio sales. They come in handy particularly when you meet people face-to-face. Carry them with you wherever you go, because you never know when you will meet someone who might be interested in your work!

Artist Postcards

Giving out postcards is a simple yet effective way to get art directors or potential customers to see your work. You can hand one out to people you meet in person and include one in every order you send out. Many art buyers and art directors keep a file of postcards they receive. You may not hear back right away after mailing one postcard, but when just the right opportunity comes along, they may contact you. Some artists send postcards three to four times a year announcing new work or shows. And even if you send out multiple cards, it's good to think of each postcard as the first impression you will make on a potential client or customer.

There are many online print labs (see Resources) that make it easy to print postcards with templates to follow, so finding one won't be too hard. Look for one with good print and paper quality at a price that you can afford. Ask them to send you samples of postcards so you can see the different paper weights and their printing methods. If you don't have an event to promote, start small with your first postcard order and keep it around a hundred. You never know when your information might change, plus redesigning your postcard every year is a great way to keep your brand fresh and show off your latest work. Here are some tips for designing your postcard:

.... *Choose images wisely.* Postcards have limited space, so you won't be able to show the complete range of your work. Use an image that's received a lot of attention or one that is in an exhibition. Ideally, place only one or two images on your postcard. Avoid making a collage of small images, since it will be difficult for the viewer to see the detail in your work. And if you do include more than one image, make sure the images complement each other.

.... *Include pertinent information.* Clearly provide your contact information including your name, email, and website address. If the piece you featured on the front was part of an exhibition or won an award, note that on the back of the card. If the postcard is announcing an upcoming exhibition, make sure the dates of the exhibition and opening party and the location are featured prominently. Keep any text brief because the main focus should be the imagery!

.... *If graphic design isn't your thing, get help.* Being an artist doesn't necessarily make you a graphic designer. If you are worried that your postcard design isn't going to show your work in the best light, enlist a designer to help you with it. If you decide to make it yourself, at minimum, ask your friends for feedback on your card before you have it printed. Can they easily find the important information? Is the image of your work strong?

Business Cards

When I moved into a career as an artist, I wondered if I would still need a business card. I learned quickly that having a business card on hand, much like in my former career, was a great way to make connections with potential customers and clients. And since they're so small, you can carry a few in your bag or wallet to share with people you meet.

The best business cards for artists are ones that feature the contact information in a clear type treatment and possibly a logo. It doesn't need to convey anything about their actual work, since postcards are often better at depicting that. Printing your card on heavy cardstock can further communicate a feeling of quality in your brand. Here are some tips for designing business cards:

.... *Use sturdy paper, like cardstock.* Don't use paper that is too thick, since really heavyweight cards may not fit well into some wallets.

.... *Keep it simple.* Business cards are small, so don't overload yours with too much information. Your email address and website URL are essential. A phone number and Twitter handle are also great if you have room.

.... *Don't use "free" business cards.* These often have advertisements on the back and this only detracts from and degrades your brand.

.... *Keep your cards updated.* Do you have a new website URL or phone number? Make sure your business cards are always current.

 WORD OF MOUTH

It is true that you never know who might be interested in your work and where you might encounter them, and there is often no better sales pitch than talking about your work and your process with people you encounter. Whenever people ask you what you do—whether you are at a birthday party, a family reunion, or sitting on the subway—talk about what you do with conviction and pride. And those postcards and business cards you had printed? Hand one over when the conversation ends.

Several years ago I was at the birthday party of a close friend. My friend introduced me to another guest by telling her I was the artist behind a piece of art in his home, which she apparently loved. Immediately her face lit up, and we engaged in a long conversation about the painting and my journey as an artist. By the end of the conversation, she'd commissioned me to make a large painting for her home. Without even trying, I made an art sale at a birthday party!

If you are not comfortable chatting with strangers in person, connections with customers can happen just as successfully online. Artists can make connections with potential customers through their Facebook fan pages or Instagram feeds. Posting photos of completed works or works in progress is a great way to generate interest in your work. Potential customers may fall in love with a piece of art and comment that they'd like to commission a piece (always read your comments!) or contact you about purchasing a specific piece.

ERIC REWITZER AND ANNIE GALVIN

Printmakers and painters

SAN FRANCISCO, CALIFORNIA

WWW.3FISHSTUDIOS.COM

In 2007, artistic husband and wife duo Eric Rewitzer and Annie Galvin opened 3 Fish Studios, a unique studio and storefront in San Francisco where they make and show their artwork and invite people to share in the joy of doing the same. Eric initially went to Michigan State to study law but learned quickly that he had no interest in the subject—his calling was in art. He left law school to attend the Cleveland Institute of Art. After finishing school, Eric continued to pursue his artistic talents while making his way through the business world and landed a position at Apple, which was his last job before becoming a full-time artist. Annie, a native of Ireland, went to art school in Waterford to study graphic design and later worked as an illustrator in a Dublin agency. When she moved to San Francisco, she spent her days working as a content strategist but, like Eric, never stopped creating art during her downtime. They met in 1998, drawn together by their dedication to art, and married in 2001. They are strong believers in collaborative process—with each other and also with people who visit their studio. They combine their love for painting and printmaking with their passion for teaching and interacting with people at their studio.

Why did you decide to open the 3 Fish Studios storefront?

Eric: At first we had a beautiful space on the third floor of an old tin can factory. But we began looking for a location where we could make and sell our work, teach classes, and host events. We are in a quiet neighborhood, which is perfect because the walk-in traffic during the week is light, so we can keep busy with our projects without a lot of interruption. The weekends are bustling with people strolling around the neighborhood on their way to the beach or as they wait for a table at a restaurant. Having a retail space has left us with the unexpected benefit of feeling very connected to our community.

What are the ways you keep customers coming back?

Annie: The personal connection. Making people feel comfortable here means they often buy artwork, and they return again and again with their parents, children, or out-of-town friends to share the experience. We also try to consistently create new work so our regulars see new things whenever they visit.

What advice do you have for artists who might be interested in starting their own storefront business?

Annie: Maybe your work is in several stores, you do well at art and craft shows, and you have a thriving online store—having your own storefront could allow you to take your business to another level. We did all of those things for many years before we opened our own storefront. We recommend getting experience in areas that lend themselves to retail first, and then taking the plunge if you think it suits you. Cash flow is a big challenge when you take on the expense of a storefront. If you get a large business space, it might mean that you'll need to hire staff to help manage it. And the rent, insurance, utilities, and other expenses may come as a shock when you transition your art business from the spare bedroom to a storefront. So we advise saving as much money as you can to get the storefront up and running, and then go for it!

Aside from the storefront, you also do online sales, wholesale sales, art shows, and events. How does all of that work together?

Annie: We have multiple revenue streams, which help keep the cash flowing. Online sales are straightforward for us; our paintings and prints show well on the web and are easy to ship. While online storefronts like Etsy are great, we made the decision early on that if people went searching for our work, we wanted them to land on our site, not someone else's. We also sell our work wholesale and get consistent orders from our shops, which is a great source of revenue.

Eric: Art and craft fairs were instrumental in getting us in front of customers when we were just starting out. We were exposed to so many other independent artists and art enthusiasts, which resulted in a lot of interest in our work. Teaching classes has always been part of our philosophy as artists and a proven business model—having new people come in every other week to learn how to do printmaking keeps people interested in us.

How do you promote 3 Fish Studios?

Eric: Aside from using social media and our newsletter, one thing that greatly helps promote 3 Fish Studios and my work as an artist is being involved in the arts community. I volunteer at ArtSpan, an arts organization in San Francisco that runs SF Open Studios. It was instrumental for

me in becoming a full-time artist, so I have been on the Open Studios Committee for the last three years. Our meetings are about more than just planning—we share information about shows, classes, events, and other opportunities that make up the fabric of the local art scene. Two years ago I joined the ArtSpan board, which connects me to the arts community even more by helping develop events to teaching the business of being an artist.

GETTING PRESS MENTIONS

One of the by-products of good self-promotion is even more promotion. There is a snowball effect: press begets more press. So if you get online press, it's just a matter of time before print press starts knocking on your door—and vice versa. And if you act as your own publicist, you can increase your chances and speed that process along, instead of waiting for that well-known blog or magazine to chance upon your work and write about it. You may be concerned that your work isn't quite ready for prime time or that writing a press release is akin to bragging. Nothing could be further from the truth! As artists, we need both feedback and validation to continually develop, and getting press is an important part of that process.

One of the first steps in doing press outreach is creating a list of blogs and magazines to contact. This will require some research, including scoping out the names of editors, along with their email addresses. You can find the names of editors in the mastheads of magazines. Look for the editor of the department that most closely matches the category for the pitch you have in mind. If it's an art magazine and your pitch is about how you recently won an award, you could contact one of the senior editors. If you want to pitch one of your new prints to a lifestyle magazine, you could contact the market editor since they normally handle products. For blogs, find the submission email on the blog's contact page.

Be sure to include your "dream" press in your list, even if you don't think it's realistic or they don't typically write about art. For instance, if your art is science-related, like abstract drawings based on a microscopic view of plants, consider pitching your work to a science magazine or blog. Like a publicist, you'll have to think creatively about different angles and publications that might be interested. Bloggers and magazine editors are more likely to write about your work if there is a compelling story. When you pitch an article, talk about the story, present a specific angle, and show images. For example, if you want a lifestyle blog to post about your home (which also cleverly displays your artwork), you need to email the editor with a brief introduction about yourself, your work, and your home along with snapshots of your space.

Always contact publications with a single pitch, one at a time (starting first with the blog or magazine you are most interested in), and move on to the next only after you've gotten a rejection or haven't heard back in a week or two. If publications are noncompeting, it's fine to contact them at the same time. For example, if you are contacting a science magazine, it's probably okay to also contact an art magazine. That said, many blogs have non-compete requirements, which means they want exclusive content, regardless of whether another blog fits in the same category. Do your research beforehand so that you comply with each blogger's requirements.

Once you've contacted an editor at a publication, wait a couple of weeks and follow up if you haven't heard anything. It's not unusual to receive a response weeks or even months later. Bloggers and journalists need time to review your pitch and make sure it's the right fit for their audience. If they pass on your first pitch, wait a couple of months before you contact the same publication with your next pitch. And make sure your pitch is about something different. Once a relationship has been developed with a writer or editor, it's important to nurture it. If you provide bloggers with good stories about your work, they will continue to write about you.

PREPARE A PRESS KIT

When press comes knocking at your door, there's often a tight deadline, so it pays to be ready. Having a press kit that is accessible on your website can make the editor's job easier. A press kit is basically a collection of documents and images that includes your contact information, any recent press releases, a bio with some background on your work, your CV, clips of recent press, and a set of images of your current artwork.

A press release is appropriate when you have something more newsworthy to announce—like the premiere of a new body of work that is a departure from your signature style, a show you will be having at a gallery, or a new set of limited edition prints supporting a charity. You can find samples of good press releases online, but here are a few necessities:

- Begin the release with FOR IMMEDIATE RELEASE at the top.

- Prominently display your contact information, including your name and email or phone number.

- Include a bold headline that summarizes the topic of the release.

- Right before the first sentence, include your city and state, along with the date.

- Try to write the press release as if it were an article in a magazine (get the help of a professional if necessary). Editors and bloggers often lift some copy directly from press releases.

- Include one to three images with your press release and a link to the place where the recipient can view your work.

ADVERTISING ONLINE

Unlike getting press or having a well-known blogger retweet a mention of your upcoming show, advertising is a marketing method where you have to pay to get your name and art in front of people. Regardless, it's another way to continue to generate interest in your work. One of the most affordable and accessible forms of advertising are banners on blogs, company websites, or organizations that write about creativity, art, design, craft, or home décor. In general, the more popular a blog and the more visible the ad—for example, in between posts, leaderboards at the top of the page, or banners above the fold—the higher the cost of the ad will be. Blogs often provide a range of advertising options, so you may be able to find a rate that works for you. You can even pay to have a sponsored post about your work and host a giveaway of one of your pieces. Blogs often have a FAQ page with information about how to get their advertising rates, so survey your favorite sites and put in an inquiry.

It's important to think strategically about when to advertise. Typically, a good time is right after you've received press mentions; your advertisement can serve as a reminder, keeping the momentum going after the press mentions fade. Another great time to advertise is when you are promoting a sale or a show. Giving people a good reason to visit your shop by offering a discount or limited edition work can help increase the chances that the advertisement pays off. The holiday season can also yield high return, as people are looking to shop for gifts and are more likely to spend a bit more money on something unique or handmade.

CREATING A MARKETING PLAN

I recommend making a marketing plan for each quarter of the year. Depending on your career goals, what you're currently working on, and the season ahead, your marketing plan will likely look different each quarter. For example, in the third quarter, when you are gearing up for the holidays, you may want to focus your marketing efforts on promoting commissions, and in the fourth quarter, you may want to organize your marketing efforts around increasing shop sales. If you're looking to launch your illustration career, you may want to do that in the first quarter, so your postcards don't get lost in the holiday mix in editorial offices. Being strategic, and not just marketing when things are slow, will serve you well in the long run.

Your marketing plan should outline the particulars of a campaign, which can include a press release, several posts on your own blog, and a big social media push. It helps to make a spreadsheet of each quarter's campaign including deadlines and tactics, along with details that become your to-do list each week of that quarter. The more organized your promotion, the more effective it will be.

SELLING *your* ART

There is nothing like the feeling of selling your artwork to a passionate buyer. These days, working artists sell their work through gallery representation, online sales, exhibitions, or commissions—or, most commonly, a combination of all four. Many artists will sell original work at least once during their career—and that includes illustrators whose work is primarily commercial. Creating print reproductions provides another way to get your work into the hands of more people at a lower price point. Whether you decide to sell original works or prints, understanding how to sell, price, pack, ship, and provide customer service will help increase sales and guarantee an enjoyable experience for your consumers—and a profitable experience for you.

SELLING PRINT REPRODUCTIONS OF YOUR WORK

Selling digital print reproductions of your original art allows you to offer your work at a lower price point and is a great way to get your work out into the world. A digital print reproduction is made from a high-resolution scan or photograph of your original artwork. It works best with work that is two-dimensional (as opposed to a sculpture or three-dimensional mixed media work), because photographs and scans of two-dimensional work look essentially the same (minus any texture). When I discuss prints in this chapter and throughout the book, I am referring to digital print reproductions and not to printing techniques like screenprinting or lino-cuts. Those are considered original works that have multiple editions.

UNDERSTANDING DIGITAL PRINTING TERMS

Take a glance through any online marketplace that sells digital print reproductions of fine art and you will see terms like "archival" and "giclée" and "limited edition." What do these terms mean and which of them apply to your reproductions? Here are some definitions:

Archival acid-free paper: Paper with acid removed from the pulp so that it has a neutral pH of 7.0 (or above). The acid that normally occurs in paper can turn it brittle or discolor it over time. Digital print reproductions or photographs printed on acid-free paper will not fade or disintegrate as rapidly.

Archival ink: UV-resistant ink is ideal for digital photo prints. Using archival ink will help prevent your prints from fading quickly over time.

Digital printing: The process of printing a digital scan or photograph with a digital printer. Nowadays, most prints that you see in the market are digital prints made from scans of original works.

Giclée: A high-quality print made by a digital process and typically printed by inkjet.

Inkjet printer: A type of printer that sprays tiny spurts of ink onto paper to create a reproduction of a digital image.

Limited edition: A number of identical artworks that are produced from a single master, all of which depict the identical image. Each print may include the artist's signature and the unique number of the specific print as well as the maximum number of prints in the edition.

Open edition: An edition or set of identical prints from a single master that is not limited in number.

Reproduction: A copy of an original work of art. In the context of digital printing, a reproduction refers to a copy of original artwork that exists in a one-off form, like a painting, drawing, or collage.

Resolution: The pixels per inch, or pixel density of your digital image. For the purposes of digital reproductions, it's crucial to scan your artwork at high resolution, which is 300 dpi (dots/pixels per inch) or higher.

Scanned image: Artwork that has been digitized with a scanner. A scanner is a piece of hardware that illuminates, reads, and then converts original artwork into digital data.

Signed print: A print that carries the original signature of the artist. Signing your prints not only ensures authenticity, but will also add to the value of the print as your work becomes more known and more valuable.

PLANNING YOUR PRINTS

There are no hard-and-fast rules for which kinds of art make great prints. The work of some artists is so popular that limited-edition prints sell out in several hours or minutes! However, if you are not yet a well-known artist, you'll want to think about which images will be the most appealing to your customers. In addition, there are some other considerations when you embark on making prints:

.... *Think about your market.* Who is your market and what would they like? For example, if you want to cater to the children's market, consider offering prints with imagery that will appeal to children and would look great in a kid's bedroom.

.... *Survey others for opinions.* Asking for objective feedback, even from your friends and family, will help you gain some perspective. You might think a piece would make a great print, but others may see it differently. If you have a blog or are active on social media, you can even casually survey your fans and followers to see if they'd like to see a particular piece of art as a print.

.... *Going for broad appeal.* Consider whether the artwork would appeal to a lot of people. Ask yourself and your friends: Is this imagery too obscure or will it have mass appeal? For example, I posted a colorful print of a drawing of beautiful chairs I had seen on a trip to Sweden. Since I loved the drawing, I was sure it would sell well as a print. After two months on my site, I sold only two! My hunch is that Swedish chairs didn't have a wide enough appeal. Conversely, I posted a print of a decorative geometric illustration of fish and sold twenty in one week alone, and many more since. Many people bought it to hang in their kitchens and others purchased it for their children's rooms. So you can consider themes that work for display in specific places in the home such as food imagery for the kitchen, baby animal prints for a nursery, or imagery that lends itself nicely to certain gift-giving occasions like Valentine's Day or anniversaries. What is it that makes your work more than just a pretty image, but a piece that someone feels they need to own?

.... *Choose the best size for the piece.* Most prints, whether you print them yourself or through a print shop, come in standard sizes prescribed by the size of the paper. And this is good, because people want to be able to place their prints in standard frames. Within the available paper sizes, choose a print size that will best highlight the artwork. Art with a lot of small details tends to look best when printed at a larger scale, like 18 x 24 inches, but some art is flexible enough to look good in a variety of sizes. If you are able, run some test prints to determine which size looks best. If you make your own prints, you can even offer prints at more than one size. Remember that the larger the print is, the more expensive it is to ship. Make sure you consider packaging and shipping costs before you invest in creating large prints.

.... *Limited versus open edition.* Whether you list prints as limited or open edition should depend on your goals. For example, if you are a fine artist who has aspirations to sell your work with a more prestigious gallery, keeping your prints at limited edition will be best, since you want to keep access to your work exclusive. Exclusivity can eventually lead to greater value down the road. But if you're simply looking to make sales, then open edition is best.

DOLAN GEIMAN

Mixed media artist

CHICAGO, ILLINOIS

WWW.DOLANGEIMAN.COM

Mixed media artist Dolan Geiman grew up in Virginia's Shenandoah Valley, exploring his native surroundings, rummaging through abandoned houses, and collecting artifacts. His childhood in the rural countryside heavily influenced his own blend of folk-meets-pop paintings and collages. Dolan attended James Madison University in Harrisonburg, Virginia, where he graduated with a BFA and shortly thereafter set off for Chicago with the goal of raising his artistic profile to a national level. Equipped with just his car, a handful of artwork, a few supplies, and a fishing pole, he began his new journey. Years later, Dolan produces a wide range of original works and print reproductions. In addition to managing an Etsy shop and participating in juried art fairs, Dolan works with international retailers that stock his original artwork as well as affordable art gifts and décor that he produces himself. He also licenses his art to companies like Anthropologie, Fossil, Pendleton Woolen Mills, and Urban Outfitters.

You unabashedly promote your work—online, in person at art fairs, and in print postcards. What's your philosophy behind selling your work and where does that come from?

My mom is an artist and I had a weird "carny" kid upbringing, traveling around doing art fairs. So making and selling art was part of my world from a very early age. My mom was good at promoting and selling her work, so I learned about the importance of connecting with people from her. She had a studio at home and would send postcards to invite people to see her work. Also, every time she got her hair done, she would give the owner some paintings for the beauty parlor. She always had artwork with her to show or sell. I was fascinated by how everyone that she met was excited to see her. She was always promoting herself and her work in a positive light. I try to emulate that. My philosophy is that if people feel a positive impact from your artwork, they'll want to have it in their lives.

You make some of your living from reproductions of your work. How did this all begin for you?

When I was in art school I explored the world of making one-off pieces, but what I never really understood was how you could make a living from one-offs alone, unless you became really famous fast. Professors would say, "Don't worry about the money." This frustrated me because it didn't seem realistic. The message I got was "You are not really an artist if you are focusing on how to make money." I wanted to make things that I loved and make a living doing it. I realized one way to make money was to reproduce my work and sell it at a price the average person could afford.

First I made screen-printed designs because I could make fifty of them at one time. After college, I moved on to printing reproductions of my mixed media work and

selling them at bigger art fairs and online.

How do you determine the best price points for your reproductions?

Obviously, you start with the base price, which is the cost that went into making the print. I experimented a lot in the beginning, making prints valued at different price points. After a few shows, I noticed that I sold everything priced at $250, but nothing at $400. $250 was my golden number. I also sell things at a lower price point, but I want them to be good quality, so I use archival-quality paper and ink.

Do you set any rules for when a piece of original art becomes a print reproduction or is licensed?

My goal isn't exclusivity, so when I make an original I also make a print right away. The main thing to remember in terms of originals becoming reproductions is to always document your original work. Take high-resolution photographs or scans, or find someone who can do it, even if you have no plans to make a print or license it immediately. Inevitably you are going to make a cool piece and sell it, and then several months or years down the line someone may want to license it. You'll want to have a large high-resolution image ready for them.

How did you get into licensing your work for home décor? And what advice do you have for emerging artists who are looking to license their work?

What people may not know is that representatives from décor companies come to art fairs to find work to potentially license. So when representatives started approaching me, I made sure to let them know I was interested. They also scour the Internet for artists, so having an online presence is important.

Artists should work with companies they like and shouldn't be afraid to ask for more money if they feel the offer is low. It never hurts to ask for more money. Keep pushing the value of your work. Licensing isn't always very lucrative, but it legitimizes you to have

a major retailer as a client. It's how you build your client list and portfolio. Licensing jobs get your work into the market. Once you are established, you can be more discerning and demand more money.

Any last tips for aspiring artists?

So many people want to be the next Warhol, but it's important not to get caught up in that. Let people see *you*. What creates success is that people like you and your story. Some people say, "I don't have a cool story," and they are shy about talking about who they are. I say, make one. Make your life your story.

CREATING DIGITAL VERSIONS OF YOUR WORK

Whether you are getting artwork ready to show in print or online, a strong, representative image is essential. A properly photographed painting or sculpture will help sell your work to press contacts, galleries, and potential customers. If you plan to do it yourself, learning to scan and photograph your work well can take time. You'll have to read your scanner and camera manuals to understand their capabilities and experiment with your equipment. Scanning is great for small, flat, lightly textured work, while photography is better for larger, heavily textured, or three-dimensional work.

Scanning Your Work

When shopping for a scanner, look for one with a large flatbed, a minimum of 9 x 12, which is a standard size. Before you use it, read your scanner's manual and familiarize yourself with the different settings. A flatbed scanner is like a copier. It has a glass plate under a lid and a moving light that scans across your art. Before each use, carefully clean the glass with a damp cloth or glass cleaner and dry. Put the artwork facedown on the glass and make sure the artwork's edges are parallel with the edges of the glass plate. Scan images in full color, except when you are scanning black on white line work, in which case scanning in grayscale or black and white is best. Scan everything at 400 dpi or more and increase your output size based on the largest size you may need for the image. For example, if you're scanning a 6 x 9–inch drawing, but think that you'd like to sell it as a 8 x 10–inch print, make sure your output size is at least that large. Start with standard scan settings, adjusting the brightness and contrast if needed. If your scanner has a setting that allows you to improve shadow separation, use it. Save your images as TIFFs, which give the best-quality image.

Photographing Your Work

If you want to photograph a flat piece of art, whether it's a work on paper or canvas, it's best to lay the piece on a flat surface or hang it on a wall, if possible—this will create the least amount of distortion. Place the artwork against a clean, simple background like a white wall or a large piece of white foam core. However, if you have art that is predominantly white or has white edges, you should place it against a darker, solid background. Choose a location to photograph your work that has soft, natural light and avoid areas where there is harsh, direct light that can cast shadows or reflections, or can change the color of your work. Shooting outdoors on an overcast day is a great option. If you are shooting indoors, turn any additional lights off, as they can cast a yellow or blue glow onto the photo. Start by setting your camera's ISO to 100 or 200, which are the best settings for natural light, and shoot with your camera's "raw" setting, which gives you the highest resolution. Do not use any flash. You can adjust the white balance on your camera, too, which allows you to compensate for the slight color differences in different types of light. For example, when the light appears too yellow in your photograph, you can whiten it using this setting. Use a tripod (along with a lateral arm, if you're photographing art on the ground) so that your camera remains as stable as possible and so your artwork is parallel to the lens of the camera. In the viewfinder, include only a small amount of space around the artwork to maximize its size. Also, make sure the image is in focus. If it's not, the autofocus feature on your camera may have made a mistake or the camera may have moved. Take several shots to choose from. (For more on photographing your work, see the interview with Julie Schneider on page 102.)

Editing Your Scans and Photos

Once your work is scanned or photographed, you will need photo editing software to retouch the photo. The most popular and comprehensive photo editing software is Photoshop, but iPhoto also has basic editing tools and there are web-based programs like Picasa, which are either low-cost or free. When you edit your scanned photo, consider the following:

- If the photo or scan is lopsided or rotated in the wrong direction, use the software's rotation tools to straighten the image and orient it properly on the screen.

- If you shot the image without a tripod and the camera lens was not parallel to the artwork, you may have an image with a perspective that is slightly askew or distorted. Photoshop has a lens distortion filter that can help correct this. It can also fix vignetting on your photo (dark corners).

- Most photos and scans need to be cropped, if just a little. Make sure that you are not cropping out any important parts of the artwork or, conversely, not leaving any area outside of the artwork in the final image.

- Take a look at the brightness and tone of the image. Does it appear too dark? Adjust the light balance so that the image on the screen appears as close to the original as possible. You can also use the software to adjust the contrast of your image if it appears washed out.

- When examining your scan or photograph, take a look at the color. Does it closely match the original work of art? If not, use the photo editing software to adjust the colors. Most photo editing programs include tools for color correction for different hues. For example, if your cyan appears too blue, you can adjust it to make it greener.

- Clean up any smudges or mistakes. The great thing about photo editing software is that you can use it to eliminate small discoloration or markings on your work. In Photoshop, the clone stamp and healing brush tools work best for this, but the editing tools differ for each program, so research and experiment with your software's tools to see what works best.

CREATING PRINTS OF YOUR ORIGINAL WORK

There are two basic ways to make print reproductions. One is to hire a printing lab to print them for you and the other is to make them yourself using a professional-grade printer and high-quality paper. There are advantages to either route; it really depends on the volume of prints you want to produce, how much of an investment you want to make in inventory or equipment, and how much time you want to spend on your print business.

Printing at a Lab

If you're starting out, work with a printing lab first. Making your own prints means investing in a large professional-quality printer, and that is a good idea only when you're selling prints regularly. There are many printing labs all over the country and even in your local community, and many operate online (see Resources). Printing labs can take a high-resolution scan or photograph of your original artwork that you provide and make a set of prints from it. Most labs will ask for a TIFF (.tif) file, so be prepared to save your file in this way. Some companies also provide the service of scanning or photographing your work for you, too; if you don't trust yourself to do it, this can be helpful. For your finished prints, they often offer different paper finishes to choose from—like matte or glossy, for example—and can send you samples. Always look at and feel the paper options. Matte paper with a thicker stock tends to show paintings and drawings in their best light. Conversely, glossy photo paper might be a more sensible choice for photographs or photo montages. It's also possible to print on textured paper, which resembles canvas or textured drawing paper.

Deciding how many prints to order can be tricky because you can never quite predict if they will be popular and sell quickly. But first, you'll need to decide if you want an open edition or a limited edition, like only twenty-five, fifty, or a hundred, for each piece of art you want to reproduce. While you'll notice that many print houses lower the price per print the more you order, if you are just starting out and experimenting with selling prints, it's a good idea to start with a smaller run like ten or twenty-five—you can always order more to complete or expand the edition.

Colors and color gradients often appear differently on a computer screen than they do on paper, so make sure that the printing lab sends you proofs to approve. If you're working with a print house across the country, this may mean waiting a few days for your proof to arrive—it's worth it. And make sure that the proof is printed on the actual paper that they'll use on the final prints. Review the colors, the print quality, and the paper before approving your order.

Making Your Own Prints

If the print-selling portion of your art business is doing well, it might make sense to invest in a professional-grade printer. The most significant reason is that having a printer allows you to print on demand—and that means you print only what you've sold. If you work with a printing lab and order fifty prints, there's a chance that you could be stuck with twenty that never sell. Making a print only when someone has purchased it will cut down on the need for inventory storage space. And you can list prints in your shop and if the image isn't popular and doesn't sell, you haven't lost any money.

Other advantages to purchasing your own printer include having more control over color adjustments and being able to easily make hundreds of prints for an open edition or wholesale orders. But making your own prints does have its hurdles and drawbacks. If you print a limited-edition print on demand, you'll have to create a system to keep track of how many you've produced. And making your own prints requires more time since you'll be managing the process yourself. In general, I carve out one morning a week for my Etsy print orders. Since I get anywhere from eight to fifty orders a week, printing can sometimes take all day. In addition, you'll need to factor in drying time, about a few minutes for each print.

Professional printers are also a significant investment, especially for a new art business. Epson, Canon, and Hewlett-Packard are the most popular brands and the cost can range from $1,500 to $10,000. But you can get a good professional-quality printer for about $2,000. On top of the machine's cost, you'll also have to buy ink regularly. For example, the Epson 3800 series requires nine ink cartridges, and each cartridge is about $60. However, the cartridges can last a fairly long time, unless you are doing a high volume of printing.

If you're ready to make the leap to printing yourself, aside from purchasing a reputable brand of printer, look for one that:

.... *Handles high-volume art or photograph printing.* You are not buying a household inkjet printer. You need one that professionals use to make archival print reproductions. Read the product description to ensure that the printer can tolerate a high volume of printing and is designed for use by professional print houses, artists, or photographers.

.... *Uses archival inks.* Archival inks prevent premature fading. With archival ink and paper, your print could last up to a hundred years or more (if it's protected against direct sunlight).

.... *Prints true colors.* Look for a printer that uses a range of ink cartridges (like the Epson 3800 series, which uses nine) and allows almost limitless colors. For most good-quality professional-grade printers, neon paint colors are the only colors that won't print looking like the original.

.... *Has good ink economy.* You don't want to be replacing ink cartridges too often. For most professional-grade printers, it's the ink cost that adds up. Research consumer reviews online to find out how much ink cartridges cost and how long they last.

.... *Can print in large format.* You'll want the flexibility to print in a variety of sizes. The Epson 3800 that I use, along with many other professional-quality printers, can print at a large size; some can produce poster-size prints (18 x 24 inches).

Ultimately, your print can be only as good as the paper you choose. You'll want to use archival-quality acid-free paper that shows your artwork's true colors and beauty. The good thing about the professional-grade printers made by Epson, Canon, and Hewlett-Packard is that those companies also make their own archival-quality papers that work well with their printers. You are not, however, limited to paper produced by the printer manufacturer. If you are adventurous, more experienced, or seeking a paper finish that your printer manufacturer doesn't offer, you can explore the wide range of digital photographic papers made by photo and fine art paper manufacturers. Visit your favorite photography store to review sample books. They may be able to give you samples to test on your printer before you commit to buying a whole box.

 ## APPLYING YOUR ART TO OTHER PRODUCTS

Before I ever delved into selling prints in my online shop, I offered notecard sets. Making cards or notebooks that feature your artwork can be very easy. Select a trusted local printer or online printing lab, like the one that makes your prints. In addition, companies like Society6 and Imagekind allow you to upload high-resolution images of your designs and place them on different products—including things like smartphone covers and pillows—and sell the products straight from their site. Regardless of where your products are printed, make sure the finish and quality are high. Many print houses—both local and online—will provide you with card and notebook samples to review before ordering. Take the time to get samples (even if it means you have to purchase one) before moving forward to ensure the print and product quality are up to your standards. (See Resources for more on printing services.)

PRICING PRINT REPRODUCTIONS

To earn back the investment on prints and to make a profit, you'll have to price them appropriately. If you have your prints made by a print lab, you can start by doubling the price you paid for each print plus the cost of any packaging like a cellophane sleeve. This will give you a starting point for your wholesale price, or the price that you offer to retailers. Double the wholesale price and you will reach your retail price, or the price that you extend to customers on your website or at art and craft fairs. If you make your own prints, itemize all the costs going into the print, including the cost of the ink, paper, packaging, and your time. Once you've reached a total cost, generate wholesale and retail prices. In both cases, if you do some research and realize your print can pull a higher retail selling price, raise it to match market values. It means a bigger markup for you—and more profit. And if the print is part of a limited edition, you can sell it for a bit more than an open edition. People are often willing to pay more money for a print of which there are only ten, twenty-five, fifty, or a hundred, as opposed to a print where hundreds have been made and sold.

PRICING ORIGINAL WORKS

If you ask any artist for tips on pricing one-off art, you might hear a large sigh. It isn't difficult, but it can stir insecurity in artists, especially those just starting out. Because art is so subjective, there is no easy mathematical formula for attaching a price tag. Ultimately, it's nothing more than an educated guess. But educating yourself is key. First, you should always start by thinking about the price based on what the work is worth, and not where the work is being sold. No matter where your artwork is sold, it should have a consistent price tag. That is, the same sculpture shouldn't bear different price tags when you're selling it online versus selling it through a shop or a gallery. Inconsistent pricing will only confuse or even anger potential buyers. Many buyers do research before purchasing artwork, and if they see that your work has disparate pricing in different venues, they may question its value altogether.

It's also helpful to understand how people who buy your art make decisions about what to purchase and how much to spend. People buy art for many different reasons—including for pure love of art, for decoration, for financial investment, or a combination of those factors. When people think about buying art, it can be a calculated decision (they are looking for a painting that fits above their credenza) or an impulsive one (they fell in love with the drawing they saw in a gallery). Either way, buyers typically purchase art based on a connection they make with the piece. The connection can be visual or something that happens when they learn the story behind the piece or artist.

To price your work effectively, you must be able to objectively evaluate the relevance or popularity of your work in relationship to the larger art market or niche in which you sit. You will also need to consider if you have a following or fan base for your work and whether they will be eager to purchase it. Obviously, if you end up working with a gallery, your gallery owner or representative will help you price your work. Here are some tips for pricing your original work:

.... *Understand the big picture of your art market.* Familiarize yourself with what other artists are creating, how their work is priced, and whether it's selling, and you'll be better prepared to price your art to sell. A good way to think about it is pricing your art the way that a real estate agent would set the price of a home. They base home prices on "comparables," or the selling price of similar houses in the same neighborhood. You can research comparables, too, by looking at artists who use similar media or sell through comparable venues, and who have similar schooling, achievements, or experience.

.... *Start low.* Once your work is priced, it's not a good idea to lower it later. While you don't want to underprice your work (people may not take you seriously if you set your prices too low), you want to start on the lower end of the going rate for work like yours. Do your research to find out what that standard price range is. When you price your work on the low end of the range, you'll be offering a competitive price that will get the work moving and into the world. More people will buy your work and that will then create a demand and a following for it. Also, when you price low to start, it gives you room to grow, and when people see that you've increased your prices, it becomes an indicator of your success. It shows that you are a rising star in the art world. If you start too high and cut your prices, it sends the opposite message.

Offer art at a variety of price points. If you offer smaller or less time-intensive pieces at lower prices, people who like your work but can't afford the big stuff will have the opportunity to buy a piece. Later, they may even come back to purchase more expensive work. Conversely, make sure there is always a more expensive option. Some art buyers are drawn to more expensive work because they are looking for pieces with prestige.

 RAISING YOUR PRICES

Once you have established a consistent and effective price point for selling your original work, there will eventually come a time when you will need to consider raising prices. The best time to up the price is when you're experiencing steady sales and you're selling at least half of everything that you produce over a six-month period. As long as demand remains high, you might consider a regular increase of your prices, like 10 to 25 percent every year. This may seem slow and cautious, but if you raise your prices too much too quickly, sales could drop off.

SELLING YOUR ARTWORK WHOLESALE

Another great way to get your work in front of a new buying audience is through a retail shop. When you sell your work to a shop, this is considered a "wholesale" account. It means that the store is buying your art in bulk, likely commodities such as prints and notebooks, at a reduced price (typically 50 percent off the retail price). The retail shop will sell the items at the retail price to make a profit. For original art, most retail shops will take your pieces on consignment and take a commission on each piece when it's sold (again, generally 50 percent of the retail price). In a consignment agreement, you maintain ownership of the artwork and if it doesn't sell, you can take it back into your possession.

If you are interested in selling your prints wholesale, contact both brick-and-mortar and online shops that might be a good fit for your work. Look at other products they carry (especially other art prints), their price points, and their overall brand. When you sell wholesale, you often give up control over the retail pricing. If you have policies about pricing—like a minimum or maximum price point or never marking down your work—make sure that the shop signs off on your requests before you make your sale to the shop. Shops often have requirements, too, like exclusivity. They may request to be the only shop in a certain geographic region to carry your products. Make sure to inquire about their exclusivity requirements for you, especially if you plan to get your work into plenty of shops in their area.

SELLING YOUR ARTWORK ONLINE

Selling works online is fast becoming the primary gateway for artists to get their artwork into the hands of buyers. Before the Internet existed, third parties like galleries or art dealers handled most art sales, even print sales! Now, individual artists can handle their own sales because so many easy-to-use and inexpensive online venues exist for artists. There are several types of online venues, including marketplaces, stand-alone store solutions, and e-commerce software. You might want to do some trial runs of different platforms to find the one that you like best.

Online Marketplaces

Think of an online marketplace as a virtual shopping mall with lots of different shops inside; popular examples include Etsy or Cargoh. For either a monthly fee or a percentage of your sales, online marketplaces provide sellers with a membership of customers and a storefront with a built-in e-commerce system that handles credit card and PayPal transactions. This is a great option if you're working on building an audience for your work. Marketplaces automatically include your shop's inventory in their searchable database and many also encourage sales by allowing members to endorse your site or pieces. For example, Etsy community members can "favorite" your shop, and Cargoh members can add your item to a wish list. Online marketplaces are also linked to social media, so it's easy for you or your customers to link to your items on Facebook or Twitter with the click of a button. While setting up your own shop in a marketplace is easy, there are a few drawbacks. For instance, you can't use your own domain name. And while you may be able to create your own banner, size is limited and all shops in the marketplace have a uniformity in presentation that can make standing out more difficult.

Stand-Alone Store Solutions

Services like Big Cartel or Shopify are stand-alone store solutions that offer one-stop shop options complete with design templates, hosting, and a shopping cart. Monthly fees are normally based on the options you choose, like how many items you want to list, the number of images per product, or whether you need inventory management. Some offer useful marketing tools or social media links to promote your products. Take advantage of any trial period so you can experiment with their options before committing. Stand-alone solutions allow you to have more control over the look and feel of your shop than a marketplace. For some, you can even use your own URL. However, unlike a marketplace, you may have to provide a credit card processor and your storefront will not have a built-in membership, so people will only find your work through your efforts to direct them there and any links they find online like in blog posts or banner ads.

E-commerce on Your Site

You can also host a shop on your existing website. You can create this by integrating e-commerce software that offers a shopping cart solution. Many of these programs also include an automatic email to customers and an inventory system. Hosting your shop on your website allows you to maintain continuous branding and keeps people on your site instead of sending them elsewhere to buy your art. Designing your shop and integrating it into your website may require a web designer or developer. Or, if your site is made with WordPress, you can use a site template that offers a shopping cart solution.

 ## PREPARING YOUR ARTWORK TO SELL ONLINE

Preparing artwork to sell online is fairly simple, but requires a keen eye. You'll want to present a good-quality scan or photograph of your artwork. You can also stage a small vignette that includes the artwork in the context of a very simple and tasteful "real life" scene, so that customers can easily see what it would be like in their own home environment. If you photograph your artwork with a camera, make sure the colors are accurate since they may appear distorted in photographs, especially if you do not use natural, indirect light. Always adjust colors using a program like Photoshop or iPhoto, since customers expect the color of their purchased artwork to be just like the image they saw online.

JULIE SCHNEIDER

Community Team, Etsy

BROOKLYN, NEW YORK

WWW.ETSY.COM

Hailing from Nashville, Tennessee, Julie Schneider is an artist, maker, writer, and teacher who has worked on the Community Team at Etsy since 2007. Her job focuses extensively on creative community-facing work—including writing and editing the How-Tuesday column on the Etsy blog, building the Craft Night and the Meet & Make programs, and the annual Craft Party across the globe, as well as many other programs, events, articles, and projects. In addition to working at Etsy, she is also an active Etsy seller with a line of handmade books and paper goods.

What should artists know about photographing their work to sell online? What specific advice do you have?

My number one piece of advice is to work on product photography. When you are selling online, the customer can't pick up your work and touch it, so you want to show your customer the details. Consider including shots that show what two-dimensional work would look like framed or with props, so people can see it within the context of a home or office environment. And use props that don't distract from what you are trying to sell.

The photos themselves should be clear and crisp. It's really important to read your camera manual, so you know how to properly use your camera and its settings intimately. For example, understand the macro setting to get detail shots that are close-up. It's also worth investing in a tripod. Use natural light when possible and plain backgrounds that don't distract from your work. Learning to use a photo-editing program like Photoshop or the photo editing tools in iPhoto is really helpful.

*Tell us about the impor-
tance of product descrip-
tions and tagging. What
aspects of product descriptions lead to sales?*

On Etsy, the main areas where you
will write copy are the product's
title, tags, and description. It's important to select keywords to use
in these areas. Think about what
the item is (painting, print, etc.),
what it looks like (color, medium,
style, etc.), its particular audience
(like children), or its theme (food,
animals, abstract, etc.). Did you
use particular techniques to create
the piece? What size is it? Why do
you think people buy your work?
What is their motivation (decoration, inspiration, etc.)?

Once you come up with a list of
keywords, use them to create your
product title and tags. The title of
your product should be different
from the title of the painting or
piece of art! If I have a painting of
a unicorn jumping over a rainbow
called "Mystical Rainbow," I would
give it the product title "Large
Rainbow Unicorn Oil Painting" to
make it more specific.

The product description is the
place where you include all the
details about the piece. I recommend using bullets in your
description to communicate key
points about your work and even
preemptively answer questions
customers might have.

You should ask a friend to read
over your descriptions to give you
feedback and to ensure you've
covered all the obvious information.
Sometimes the most obvious desc-
riptors are the ones we leave off!

*What other tips do you have
for artists selling their work
on Etsy?*

Artists should also think about the
other ways that their work can be
used on other products, like journals, dishware, phone cases, or tea
towels. If you are selling original
works alongside reproductions
and other products, it allows for a
range of prices and draws different
eyes to your shop at a variety of
entry points.

What tips do you have about pricing artwork?

I always advocate for people pricing their work at minimum to cover the time and materials. Not "underselling," or pricing your work too low, is really important, not just out of respect for yourself and your own work, but out of respect for the entire community of artists. We want artists to get to the point where they can make a living from selling their work. That won't happen if artists are coming from a perspective in which they think their work has little value or that the only way to sell it is to price it below its value.

Fine-tuning your pricing is the key to successfully making money from your artistic skills. It's not just about covering your material costs; there's a lot of time and overhead that goes into making your creations. Make sure to document all the time, raw materials, and supporting costs that go into making your art and factor them in as you develop pricing.

Is there a difference in how artists should approach selling original work versus print reproductions?

The most important thing is to be really clear about what is original and what is a reproduction. You'd be surprised how often customers are confused, thinking they are buying an original when it's actually a reproduction! In your tags and descriptions, be sure to include the words "print," "reproduction," or "original artwork."

TAKING COMMISSIONS

Do you enjoy making art that is specifically for other people? If you do, then taking commissions may be a good source of income for you. Buyers normally request a commission when they like your work and want you to make something special for them. Most of the time commission clients give you some art direction (like a portrait of their dog) or very specific requirements (like exact dimensions for the art that will go in their hotel lobby) or both.

Commissions come with some risk. Since the client often agrees to begin paying you before they have seen the finished work, it can create the expectation (and related pressure) that they should like the work when it's finished. It's perfect for artists who like working with people and the challenge of creating art within constraints—much like commercial illustration work.

When you take a commission, you are entering into a business relationship with your client. Your ability to communicate with your customer will ultimately determine if your commission is successful. The relationship works best when you listen and respond to your client's concerns and requests. You'll need to determine your commission policies and make sure your client understands and agrees to them before you begin. Here are some areas to cover in a written agreement:

.... *Price structure and purchase policies.* What is the price of the commission and what does it include? How will the client issue payment? If the client isn't happy with the finished piece, are they obligated to pay the complete fee? Outlining the price, payment type, schedule, and purchase policies will give structure to the process and prevent any undue heartache for you or your client. It's common to require a nonrefundable advance payment of a third to a half of the total cost from the client. This way your work will not be completely in vain if the client isn't happy in the end.

.... *Time frame for completion.* Set a delivery date that is realistic, to which both you and the client agree. For example, the client may want the piece delivered in one month, but if you know your workload and process will require two months, make sure the client agrees to your timeline before proceeding. If the commission is time- and labor-intensive, you can even have the client view it in progress if you are comfortable with receiving feedback during the process.

.... *Art direction.* In the beginning, you should request written direction from the client about what they want. Asking questions like "Which of my previous works resonates most with you?" or "What specific subject matter would you like to see?" will help zero in on what the client wants if she's unable to verbalize on her own. Ask for reference material, color preferences, and anything they'd like added before you get started. And always ask clients to provide high-resolution images for portrait commissions. The more information you can get up front, the easier the process and the happier the customer will be.

PACKING YOUR ART FOR SHIPMENT

Once you've sold a piece, keeping your artwork in pristine condition as it travels to its new owner is crucial. Especially for large prints and original artwork, build room into your shipping cost to cover materials like boxes, packaging filler (like peanuts or shredded paper), and bubble wrap. You can buy materials from your local packaging store if you're shipping only a few pieces infrequently. But when you begin to ship more regularly, consider purchasing your supplies in bulk from online shipping supply sources. If you determine ahead of time how much shipping supplies and fees will cost for each piece, you can pass that cost on to the buyer in the shipping and handling fee. And finally, don't forget to put the sales receipt or invoice along with a postcard or business card in the shipment.

Unframed paintings, print reproductions, and drawings on paper:

- Place the artwork on sturdy acid-free cardboard or foam core about the size of the work or larger.

- Fold four pieces of acid-free paper into triangles with one side open, then place the triangles on each corner of the work attached to the cardboard or foam core.

- Place it in a plastic sleeve or wrap it in acid-free paper.

- Sandwich the wrapped artwork between two pieces of cardboard and tape along all four sides.

- Place it in a rigid or padded mailer and inscribe or add a "Do Not Bend" sticker on the package.

Framed artwork or works on panels or canvas:

- Use a box that can accommodate at least four inches of space on all sides of the artwork.

- Wrap the artwork with acid-free paper. You can also add cardboard corner protectors on top of the paper-wrapped artwork.

- Add a layer of bubble wrap, ensuring adequate coverage on the corners and edges.

- In the box, place packaging filler in the space between the artwork and the edges of the box. The more snug the fit, the less potential for damage.

Sculptures or fragile, oddly shaped three-dimensional works:

- Use a box in which the sculpture will fit comfortably with four to six inches of space on all sides.

- Place ample bubble wrap around the entire sculpture, wrapping at least two times around, and secure it with packaging tape.

- Fill a third of the box up with packaging filler. Set the sculpture down in the middle and fill the remainder of the box with packaging filler so no movement can occur.

- For heavy sculptures, place this box within a larger box, filling the area around the inner box with more packaging filler.

SHIPPING CARRIERS

You don't need to go with just one carrier for all your needs. You'll learn that some carriers might be better and cheaper for small packages while others are better for big shipments. Some carriers might be less expensive for international shipments as well. It requires research and getting online price quotes to determine which carrier is ideal. For example, I learned that shipping larger, heavier artwork that wasn't fragile was best accomplished through ground shipping; shipping smaller packages was most convenient through the regular postal service; and lightweight or fragile packages sent through an expedited method gave more peace of mind because they weren't in transit as long.

When you ship more expensive or fragile work, it's a good idea to insure it for its value. Some carriers automatically insure all packages for $100, so if your art is worth more than that, you'll need to pay the additional fee to cover the full value of the piece. Insurance protects you if you have to refund money to a customer because the piece never arrives or has arrived damaged. Regardless of the carrier you use, pay for tracking information or delivery confirmation when shipping original artworks, and provide this information to your customers.

If you have a piece that is particularly large, cumbersome, fragile, or expensive, it's often a good idea to hire a professional to pack or crate it. Some shipping services will come to your location to package your work and ship it. Other services may require you bring the work to their office instead. Call around for quotes to see which is the most cost-effective option for you. If the business has been reviewed online, see if they have a strong and positive reputation. Handing your artwork over to others to ship can be worrisome, but in the hands of the right people, it will save you from the heartache of art damaged in transit.

CUSTOMER SERVICE

Regardless of how you sell your work, making sure your customers are happy—individuals, galleries, and retail shops alike—will make or break the overall success of your business. Good customer service includes providing correct information to your customers, outlining your purchase policies, and communicating well with customers.

.... *Provide an accurate description.* Make your product descriptions clear and accurate to prevent situations where customers feel duped by their purchase. This also curtails emails with simple questions about the work's materials, size, and dimensions.

.... *Establish distinct policies.* Articulate a return policy that covers what types of returns you accept and the time frame to receive them. Also outline a shipping policy that states which day or days you ship, so that customers know when to expect their order, and if you cover against loss and damage.

.... *Communicate with your customers.* Answering customer service emails quickly and with a polite and positive attitude will assure your customers that you care not only about the quality of the product, but also their happiness with their purchase.

CHAPTER

5

EXHIBITIONS
and GALLERIES

Exhibiting your art is one of the most exciting and important aspects of your career. There are many ways to exhibit your work—through gallery representation, in invitational group shows, by entering juried shows, and even by creating your own exhibition. Regardless of whether you have aspirations to become a gallery artist—that is, an artist who sells original works through a gallery or set of galleries as his or her main source of income—or you only occasionally exhibit your work, understanding exhibitions and the gallery world will help you to effectively plan ahead for opportunities and make smart decisions. Showing your work through a venue, large or small, is decidedly different from selling your work on your own through an online shop—you are automatically engaged in a business relationship with the venue owners or curators. Money, contracts, and commissions will come into play, so understanding how all of these things work will be critical for your success.

JURIED SHOWS

Juried shows are excellent opportunities to build your résumé. They allow for emerging artists to enter the art world, even as unknowns. "Juried" means you must submit slides or photographs (and sometimes actual work) to be reviewed by a jury (usually a knowledgeable committee of curators or fellow artists). A select group of artists are accepted into the show based on factors like technical skill, the medium, conceptual creativity, and other requirements. Often the name of the artist is withheld from the jurors so that the selection process is unbiased. If the show offers any prizes, the jurors also select the winners. There is usually a non-refundable fee to enter, regardless of whether or not your work is selected. If you are interested in entering a juried show or you have received an invitation to enter one, be sure to do your due diligence before paying the fee and sending your artwork. Is the show long-standing and with a reputable gallery or institution? Who are the jurors? What artists have been featured in the past? Some juried shows have specific requirements about the work that will be accepted or even about the artists themselves. Make sure to research the theme of the show and requirements to gauge whether it is a good fit for you and your work.

Juried shows are excellent opportunities to build your résumé.

Some gallery artists stop entering juried shows once they are more established, participating only when they are directly invited to show. However, if you are an emerging artist, the right juried shows can offer valuable entries on your CV and a great way to expose your work to a new audience.

To find a juried show in your area, look for websites that collect and share information about open calls for shows (see Resources). Since most arts organizations list their calls on their website, a simple Internet search for the name of your town or geographic region, along with the words "juried art show" or "call for artists," can assist you in finding opportunities.

EXHIBITION INVITATIONS

An email arrives in your inbox with a subject line that reads, "You are invited to participate!" It's an invitation to be a part of a show! Exhibition invitations are some of the most exciting emails you will receive. Most often these invitations are for group shows, but occasionally they are for solo shows. Sometimes invitations, especially from larger, more established institutions, will come in a more formal manner through regular mail. A few years ago, I received an invitation to participate in a show at the Contemporary Jewish Museum in San Francisco. Even though the large envelope was addressed to me, I almost didn't open it because I wrongly assumed it was promotional materials for the museum. (I'm glad I did open it because it was the most prestigious show I'd ever been invited to participate in.)

As with juried shows, unless the gallery or curator is familiar to you, it's important to do your research before agreeing to do the show. Who's holding the show? What shows have they held in the past? What artists have they shown? Where is the shop or gallery located? If it's not clearly stated, inquire about the show's requirements—for example, how many pieces you'll need to provide, how long you have to complete the pieces, and what their commission rate is if the work sells. You should also inquire about whether they are insured for potential theft or damage and whether they install and de-install the show or if that's your responsibility.

If you are asked to submit fees, be cautious and make sure you research thoroughly what the fees will be used for. Sometimes when you are working with a nonprofit or artist-owned and -operated gallery, some fees of up to a few hundred dollars a year are generally normal. They use the fees to fund the operation and care for the gallery. However, be wary of private for-profit galleries that charge for participation in group or solo shows. Many of these galleries are scams, with empty promises of promotion, sales, exhibits, fame, and glory for a price.

All the information you gain in your research will help you make a decision about whether you can accept the invitation. Even if you need to decline, make sure to let the gallery know. You may want to work with them in the future, so it's good to keep the relationship cordial.

When you agree to participate in a show and your work is for sale, the shop or gallery will be accepting your art on consignment. Consignment means they are simply selling your work on your behalf and taking a commission (normally 50 percent) on all sales. This does not give them exclusivity over your work; you can show your work with other galleries without their involvement or expressed permission. Shops and galleries often use contracts for consignment. This kind of contract typically specifies the work that is on loan; the dates of the loan; whether your work is insured; and if a work sells, how long the gallery has to pay you. If a shop or gallery does not offer you a consignment contract, you can draw one up. It is good to get everything in writing in case anything goes awry or a gallery fails to pay you. (For more on consignment, see page 99.)

CREATING YOUR OWN EXHIBITION

Instead of waiting for a gallery or shop to come calling, create your own solo or group show in a café, restaurant, boutique, hair salon, small gallery, lobby, or even your own studio! Getting your work into a space and putting it up for sale is a helpful way to see which pieces are popular and which price points are effective. The more your work is in the public eye, the greater chance you have at becoming a bold-faced name in the art market.

First, you need to decide if you want to do a solo or group exhibition. While a one-person show might look better on your résumé, a group show has the potential to bring greater attendance (since each artist comes with their own set of fans, friends, and family) and the work and cost of putting together a show can be shared among all the participants.

When you consider venues, scout locations that have previously had art shows you've enjoyed and are a good fit for your work. Cafés, shops, and salons are great locations because they often have empty walls and are looking for ways to fill them and they are often excited at the prospect of hosting an art show. Talk to the venue about how you can mount art in their space and whether the art can be insured while it's there. The venue's availability will determine the dates of your show; typically, art shows last one to two months. Popular venues fill their exhibition space quickly and far in advance, so you may need to act fast to get your show in their lineup. When you are scheduling with the venue, make sure you or the other artists have an ample lead time to make enough work to fill the space.

One of the most enjoyable parts of putting together a show is determining its theme and title. This is your chance to curate. You'll need to choose a theme that's flexible enough to allow each artist to express himself in a way that feels natural, but also structured enough to create a cohesive collection. If you are stumped about choosing the theme, research other group shows and their themes to provide a seed of inspiration for you.

> *One of the most enjoyable parts of putting together a show is determining its theme and title.*

Next, you'll have to look for artists who would fit well within the theme and invite them to submit a few pieces (typically one to three) for consideration. Include artists who have an existing audience for their work to help your show draw a crowd. You can also put out a call for submissions on one of your local websites. When you have a theme and a proposed list of artists (if you're putting together a group show), you should approach the venue with a written description of the theme and a list of the artists and images of their work. Once your proposal is accepted, you will work with the venue to schedule the show and finalize the roster of artists. You'll also be responsible for contacting the artists with the details and deadlines, as well as any tasks they may have for the installation and opening.

In a group show, in your role as the show coordinator, you'll be acting as the venue liaison, allotting space to each artist, and overseeing the installation and removal of the exhibit. Since putting together a show is quite a bit of work, make sure to have your bases covered. Does the venue take care of any of the responsibilities? Can you cover any additional responsibilities yourself or will you need to ask the other artists participating in the show to help? Tasks required to put together a show include creating the show signage and labels with pricing for each piece of art; designing the exhibition announcement and email blast; managing the marketing and publicity for the show, including overseeing the Facebook invitation page, printing and distributing postcards, writing the press release, and contacting local blogs and publications with information about the show; and, last, arranging the details of the opening reception including bringing food, wine, and music to the event. For solo shows, you can enlist kind friends and family to help you with these tasks.

Of course, the most important job that everyone involved shares in is promoting the show! Encourage all the artists to create a buzz early on. Each artist can write about the work they are making for the show on their blog or share photos on Instagram to generate interest. Ask the artists to carry postcards to hand out when they meet people, or leave them at local cafés and art spaces. And all the artists should invite their friends to the event via a Facebook invitation. All this effort will help populate the opening and encourage people to stop by while the show is up.

JESSICA SILVERMAN

Gallery owner
Jessica Silverman Gallery

SAN FRANCISCO, CALIFORNIA

WWW.JESSICASILVERMANGALLERY.COM

Jessica Silverman began her career by studying studio art as an undergraduate at Otis College of Art and Design but quickly realized that her interests lay more in organizing and connecting the work of other artists than in making her own work. After college, she enrolled in the curatorial practice program at California College of the Arts (CCA). In 2006, during her final year as a student at CCA, she opened the Jessica Silverman Gallery. In 2013, Jessica moved to a new, larger location in San Francisco. In her role as gallery owner, Jessica has become not only an art dealer, but also curator, writer, world traveler, and "mom" to her roster of artists. Jessica seeks artists who have a strong combination of passion, talent, and drive. And her eye for emerging talent has been outstanding: works by gallery artists have been acquired by the Tate museums, Museum of Modern Art, Los Angeles County Museum of Art, Hammer Museum, Whitney Museum of American Art, San Francisco Museum of Modern Art, and the British Art Council.

What type of work do you show?

We show a lot of abstraction and hyperrealism. I have a few artists who still do figuration and landscape. Increasingly, I'm interested in artists and their relationship with the overconsumption of images. Because of technology, access to imagery is changing the way artists make work. We show video, sculpture, photography, painting—all media.

How do you go about finding new artists?

We are a staff of three, and so there is a limit to the number of artists I can represent. We don't have a submission process at the moment because we don't have the capacity to store submission materials or review all of them. We participate in art fairs, and that is a great way to find new talent. I also go to art school open studios. Much of how I find artists is by word of mouth; people who I trust call me and say, "You have to see this artist's work."

What questions do you ask yourself when you are considering a new artist?

I am looking for visually innovative and conceptually rigorous work. I am also looking for a practice. When I walk into an artist's studio, I ask myself: Do I see new materials? Do I see the artist pushing her practice and work in new and different directions? Are things moving? I look at work over a period of a year before I officially represent someone. I like to include the artist in a group show or two to see how it is to work with him first. Typically I show only full-time artists because it means they have a level of seriousness about their practice. And if they have a job, I prefer that their job is in teaching art or in the art world.

What do you expect from artists once they join your roster?

Showing in a gallery is serious business. To stay on the roster, my artists have to step up to the plate in a big way and show a commitment to growing their work. I need to be able to walk into their studios and see a full body of work and simply help edit it, as opposed to helping them develop it from scratch. We need to be able to have a conversation about their work that involves criticism and dialogue. I am looking for a confidence and conviction about their work.

What do you take into consideration when pricing the work of your artists?

I'm slow and deliberate. If artists have sold paintings out of their studio for $2,000, then we start with that price and go from there. Pricing is tough, even for more expensive work. For example, let's say there are twenty people bidding on a piece at an auction, but the last ten bids are between only two people and thousands of dollars separate those two people from the rest of the bidders. Does that mean the piece really has the higher value when only two people were ready to pay that much? These are things to watch out for. Keeping work at a reasonable price is important, because if you raise the price too quickly, you run the risk of overpricing and not selling. Once you go up, you can't go down. There are markers for raising prices; a big show at another gallery, a museum show, or acquisition by a museum would be a good time.

How do you see your role with the artists you represent?

We make sure our artists are feeling good and taking care of themselves because if they are not, they will not have a thriving studio practice. I feel like their promoter. I do their public relations. I write their press releases. I speak on their behalf. I try to communicate about their work the same way they would and that requires that I get to know them, their motivations, their inspirations, and their materials as well as they do. Gallery owners are maternal figures,

colleagues, friends, and therapists. We are also the bank!

What advice do you offer to artists who want to break into galleries?

If you are in school, ask your teachers for art gallery and curator recommendations. There is a generosity among people in the art world. And that is really helpful because the art world can feel very insular. It's also a good idea to have a strong web presence and to learn to edit the image selection of your work.

Keep your artist statement brief and to the point. Go to gallery shows. When you are there, introduce yourself to the gallery owner and let them know that you like what they do. Ask the gallery owner for a studio visit. Come to an opening. Be part of the community. Go to lectures and talks. Curate your own shows. Find the space or an artist-run gallery and organize a show. Invite people to come; invite gallery owners to come.

BIG GALLERY DREAMS

For many artists, gallery representation is the apex of their career aspirations. But new artists are like anyone else beginning a profession: they don't land their dream job right off the bat. Sure, you might hear of a bright, young artist signing with a prestigious gallery right out of school and selling work for thousands of dollars—but that's a rarity.

It's important to understand that most well-known galleries do not select artists based on who walks through their door or sends them an email. Galleries also don't select artists based solely on whether they like their work. Your work has to be just the right fit for the gallery and the collectors they serve. What may be good for one gallery may not work at another. Galleries also look at how established you are, how likely your work is to sell, and any past exposure you've had, like press or previous shows at other galleries. Use the checklist below to consider whether you're gallery-ready:

.... *Exposure.* Have you shown your work continuously over the course of several years? Have you gradually worked up from smaller venues to more established ones? Have you been included in any juried shows or won awards in any competitions?

.... *Sales.* Do you have a strong and consistent track record of selling your work? Have you been able to increase your prices over time because of a higher demand for your work? Is there a collector base for your work?

.... *Press.* What has been written about your work? Have you gotten any print or online press that has lauded or endorsed your work?

.... *Innovation.* What about your work is different from what is already in the market? How has your work developed or changed over time? Galleries are often looking for artists who continually push boundaries and explore new territory in their work.

INTRODUCING YOURSELF TO A GALLERY

Your first real step toward gallery representation is getting an appointment with or a studio visit from a reputable gallery owner. However, securing that appointment or studio visit can feel like a difficult and mysterious process. Many galleries don't provide submission guidelines. There are no set rules about how to make a connection happen because every gallery operates differently. That said, there are some general things you can do to increase the chances that your work will be seen by a gallery owner, which will further increase the chances that you sign with one. Emerging artists can sometimes make their initial contact with a gallery through an existing relationship, like a college professor or a colleague. If you went to art school, talk to your professors and administrators to see whether they might be able to connect you with someone who would be interested in your work.

Getting involved in your local arts community can also be an effective way to build relationships that could ultimately lead to representation. Show up to the openings of other artists or at galleries you admire! This is an opportunity not only to support other artists, and see the gallery system at work, but also to meet and network with other artists and gallery owners. Make it a goal to talk to the gallery owner and introduce yourself. You might also consider interning or volunteering at a local gallery, nonprofit arts organization, or museum. By being involved in your community, you are demonstrating your desire to participate. It's also a great way to make connections with people who have influence in the art world.

Mostly, remember to be patient. It can be difficult to land an appointment or garner a studio visit from a gallery owner because popular galleries are often inundated with artists' inquiries and submissions. It could take weeks or even months to hear a reply to your inquiry. But no matter how impatient you may feel, one rule of thumb: never drop in to show your portfolio unannounced.

LANDING A GALLERY APPOINTMENT

If you are fortunate enough to get an appointment with a gallery, it's important to go into the meeting as prepared as you possibly can be. Remember, galleries are not just looking for beautiful or innovative art. They are looking for people who take their work seriously and are easy to work with.

Since gallery owners are typically busy people, you may get only a very limited time for your meeting. They may call for an appointment in their gallery or choose to do a studio visit to see your work firsthand. In either case, inquire ahead of time about how long the meeting might be. Be prepared for as little as thirty minutes. It's important to walk into a review with your best work to show. Limit it to a number that allows you to present your body of work in an efficient, thorough manner. (See "Preparing Your Portfolio," page 128).

Galleries are also looking for people who are professional and can talk easily and intelligently about their work. Preparing talking points that list the key points about your work ahead of your meeting and practicing in front of friends can help. You may have only one chance to discuss your work with a gallery, so it's critical that you come across as confident and invested in your career. Print a copy of your curriculum vitae, or CV, and artist statement on résumé paper and include your contact information. After your portfolio meeting, always follow up with a thank-you note or email expressing your gratitude and interest.

SIGNING WITH A GALLERY

Congratulations—a gallery wants to sign you! But before you pop the bubbly and sign the contract, make sure the gallery is the right fit for you. Although a gallery may want you, gauge how comfortable you feel with the relationship. Do your research before you join their roster, including contacting artists who currently work with the gallery. Has their experience been positive? What advice do they have for you? If you feel good about the opportunity and you've done your research, read the contract well before you sign and understand what terms are dictated, including the commissions and fees associated with representation. Contracts are legally binding. Do not sign one unless you agree to and are willing to live with everything in it. You might want to consider asking an intellectual properties lawyer or someone who intimately understands art gallery contracts to look it over for you, too.

Representation Contract

When a gallery wants you to show exclusively with them and manage the sale of your work and your relationships with other galleries, museums, or dealers, they will usually provide a contract that outlines the terms of this relationship. Standard contracts normally cover the following:

- The percentage of commission on sales, which is typically 50 percent.

- That you own your work until your work is sold and that the gallery is working on your behalf.

- That you retain ownership of the copyright to your work and have the right to reproduce it at will, unless specified.

- The geographic region within which the gallery represents you and your work. Sometimes this is worldwide, nationwide, or limited to a specific region, like a city or state.

- That your art is covered by insurance for loss or damage while it is in the hands of the gallery.

- If a work sells, the amount of time the gallery has to pay you.

- How to terminate the relationship.

Gallery Commissions

It's exciting to get notification that a gallery has sold a piece of your work. Since galleries house your work within their walls and work on your behalf to sell it to collectors, they earn a commission from the sale price. In addition to talking about and promoting your work to potential buyers, they also handle the sales transaction and package and ship the work. Most galleries take a 50 percent commission, but some emerging galleries or retail shops with a small gallery component may take slightly lower commissions like 30 to 40 percent.

 ART FAIRS

Art fairs are fundamental venues for artists at the highest levels as well as for artists looking to break into the more prestigious realms of the art world. Fairs like Art Basel in Miami, ArtPad in San Francisco, and Frieze Art Fair in London provide unique opportunities for galleries from all over the world to come together and introduce the work of their artists to collectors, dealers, and even other galleries. Major art fairs should not be confused with smaller art and craft fairs in which individual artists and craftspeople show and sell their work. Galleries—not individual artists—show at major art fairs, so participating usually requires gallery representation. Booths can cost tens of thousands of dollars, so it's a large financial investment for a gallery. But these fairs attract twenty thousand to forty thousand international visitors, so galleries see more potential clients in several days than they do at their home gallery in a year.

Even if you don't yet have the opportunity to exhibit your work in an art fair with a gallery, attending one is a great way to learn more about what kind of artwork is in the market, how it's priced, and how art fairs operate. It's also a good way to survey galleries that might be a good fit for your work and make contact with gallery owners. The general public can attend most art fairs for a reasonably priced entry fee.

MARK HEARLD

Illustrator and mixed
media artist

YORK, ENGLAND

WWW.MARKHEARLD.CO.UK

British fine artist and illustrator Mark Hearld was born in York, England, in 1974. A consuming fascination with plants and animals stemming from his childhood is at the heart of his work. After secondary school Mark went to the Glasgow School of Art to study illustration and later received a master's degree in natural history illustration from the Royal College of Art. He works across a variety of media, including collage, printmaking, painting, and drawing, and has had solo exhibitions at various galleries and museums, including Yorkshire Sculpture Park and Scarborough Museum. He has also designed textiles and wallpapers for St. Jude's in London and completed commissions for the publisher Faber and Faber and the Tate museums. In 2012, Mark illustrated his first children's book, *Outside Your Window: A First Book of Nature,* and Merrell Publishers published *Mark Hearld's Work Book,* a book devoted entirely to his work.

Did you pursue being a professional artist right after you finished your first illustration degree?

I had a great time at Royal College of Art but felt everyone was so good. In a way I lost confidence in my abilities because it felt competitive. It took me going out on my own for about a year to begin to feel confident. I had an exhibition in a café in York. It went very well and a gallery owner from the gallery Godfrey and Watt saw my exhibition and asked me if I'd like to have some pieces in a group show in his gallery. And that was really how my career kicked off.

One of the key things I did right out of school was get into a rhythm of making work for myself. Some people imagine they can just get in with a gallery straight away after school, but it's more about being the artist you want to be before you get to that stage. The secret is finding what is particular to you, developing an individual visual language, and pursuing it rigorously.

You had a solo exhibition called The Magpie Eye in a room at Scarborough Museum. How did you come up with the concept for it?

It was an exhibition that ran along an exhibition of the work of Edward Bawden and Eric Ravilious, British artists and designers I admire. I am interested in the idea of popular art and folk art. I own a book called *Collectors' Items from the Saturday Book*, which features objects that I've enjoyed. And I thought, Wouldn't it be amazing to make an exhibition of objects displayed for their visual merit alongside my artwork? I got this idea to make a room full of covetable objects. I used things like old toys, a stuffed flamingo, a dresser full of decorative plates—all the things that I really love. My artwork was featured to complement the objects. In a way, what I made there was a three-dimensional collage.

What were the challenges of creating an exhibition at a museum?

Working with museums is not always easy. They are institutions that have certain ways of doing things. You want to move past the red tape that gets in the way of your creative freedom. You want to have your own personal stamp on an exhibition. So I worked hard to build a relationship with the people at the museum so that they would allow me to make a space that looked as though only my hands had touched it, as if it wasn't a museum display. What I've tried to do in the museum context is give the look of an artist's hand.

How did you come to design merchandise for the Tate museums in London?

In York, we have an antiquarian book fair and I designed all the ephemera, like the tickets, the posters, and the banners. The head of publishing at the Tate came to the fair and saw the ephemera. He initially wanted me to work on a book project at the Tate, but instead, I ended up designing a range of merchandise. The head of merchandise gave me free rein to come up with some ideas for products. I designed a cup, a plate, and a bowl. I was really particular about detail, even the back stamps on the plates. I went to an area in Britain that specializes in pottery production and I spoke to the makers to learn as much as I could. If you design something, especially for a product, it's important to design for each particular artifact, rather than making an image and plastering it on everything.

Tell us about Mark Hearld's Work Book. What was your goal in creating it?

The *Work Book* was this idea of a visual way of life. Because I have done so many things as an artist, the publisher thought it would be interesting to make a book that explored the depths of my interests. I worked alongside the designer on every spread. The book is about my visual inspiration and the importance of a playful approach to creativity. It's laid out like a collage so that the spreads are surprising, layered, and dynamic.

Your world and work as an artist is so diverse, from book publishing and printing to original works and creating exhibitions. What is it like having such a lively and varied career?

I feel like I am living the dream job. There isn't much of a divide between my life and my creative world. At the moment I am making a collage called *Autumn Work Table* that's going into an exhibition. I've just designed a beer label for an artisan brewery. I'm working on a jacket for a book called *Cider with Rosie*. I also teach a fundamentals class at the art college in Hull. So I have a lot of things happening at any given moment. And sometimes it can get a little bit hairy with timing because as I've gotten more established, people want more things from me. But I love the diversity of my career despite the occasional pressure.

PREPARING YOUR PORTFOLIO

When preparing your portfolio to share with a gallery, include about twenty images that show good breadth. Make sure your work is thematically cohesive to demonstrate your readiness to exhibit. If you have two or more bodies of work, consider showcasing small selections of each and make sure the first one you share is your strongest. You might also research the tastes and interests of the gallery and show the work you think would be the best fit. The order in which your work appears should make sense, either chronologically or by evolution of the work if it has changed over time. Lastly, make sure to find out how the gallery would like to see the images of your work—in a slideshow on your laptop or iPad or printed on paper in a physical portfolio. If your work is small or on paper, they may want to see original samples as well.

YOUR CURRICULUM VITAE

A curriculum vitae, or CV, is an overview of your artistic professional history and achievements. It looks similar to a résumé. A CV is important if you are interested in breaking into the fine art world or securing representation with a gallery, but less so for illustration or licensing careers. Your CV should be neatly organized and include only information pertinent to your artistic career. If you are just starting out and have very little information to include on your CV, it's okay. Begin by writing one for where you are now and you'll learn which areas you need to build or expand on. As you develop your career, continually update your CV with new information.

Sections in a CV

1. **Personal information:** The first lines in your CV should include your personal information: your name, date of birth, and contact information.

> Anna Johnson (b. 1980)
>
> info@ajohnsonartist.com | http://www.ajohnsonartist.com | 555.555.1234

2. **Education:** Generally, this section relates to your formal education, specifically in the field of art, listing the school, the year that you graduated, and the degree you earned.

> University of California Los Angeles, Master of Fine Arts in Painting and Drawing, 2010
>
> California College of the Arts, Bachelor of Fine Arts in Visual Studies, 2003

If you do not have a degree in art, don't worry—you can list your degree or simply leave this section off of your CV. This section is not a prerequisite for gallery representation or inclusion in exhibitions. Many successful artists never went to school to study art.

3. **Exhibitions:** List your exhibition history with the most recent first. If you have a number of exhibitions under your belt, you can split them into two categories: solo exhibitions and group exhibitions. Artists who have done many shows often list "selected solo exhibitions" and "selected group exhibitions," which means they are listing only the most pertinent ones. Likewise, you can weed out any exhibitions that are no longer relevant to your career.

> 2014 *Home on the Range*, Meyers Gallery, Austin, TX (solo exhibition)
>
> 2013 *While They Were Sleeping*, Faber Gallery, New York, NY (group exhibition)

4. **Bibliography:** In this section, include any articles or books in which you or your art have appeared or were reviewed. For articles, list the author, title, publication, volume, publication date, and page number.

> Johanson, Mark: "This Year's Best Emerging Artists," *Art Magazine*, vol. 10, March 2011, pp. 12–14

If a discussion of your own artwork or your artwork itself appears in a book, the formatting should include the author, title, publisher, copyright date, and page number.

> Abramson, Louise, *New Paintings in Neon*, Peacock Press, 2008, p. 20

5. **Collections:** If your work is part of a collection in any public institutions, like museums, corporate collections, municipalities or agencies, this is the section in which to list them.

> The Joseph Brink Gallery, Minneapolis
>
> The Bean Collection, Los Angeles

6. **Awards and Grants:** If you received any awards and grants related to your artistic practice, note them here.

> Finalist, New American Paintings, 2012
>
> Recipient, Southwest Emerging Artist Grant, 2011

CVs can also include additional sections, for instance teaching jobs, residencies, and writing you've done about your own work.

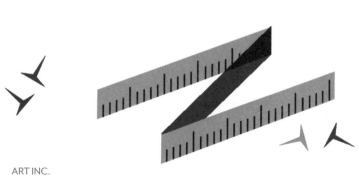

WRITING YOUR ARTIST STATEMENT

In chapter 3, we discussed writing your bio for your website or promotional materials. While your bio is a casual description of who you are and your artistic journey, your artist statement is a more formal account of your artwork, written in the first person. Your statement is a basic introduction to your work; it shouldn't be instructions on how people viewing your work should experience it. People who look at your art will inevitably have their own opinions, but they will also have questions. When you're not there to answer them, your artist statement gives people more information about what you've created.

Your artist statement should be about two to five paragraphs long and written in simple, straightforward language. People interested in your work are not necessarily immersed in the art world or scholarship, so avoid jargon or academic language. An effective statement welcomes people to your work, no matter how little they know about art to begin with. Here are some examples of topics covered in artist statements:

- ☼ What your work means to you

- ☼ What materials you use

- ☼ Your process for making your work

- ☼ What inspires your work or your latest body of work

- ☼ What your work represents

ILLUSTRATION *and* LICENSING

In the world of art, illustration holds a special place. What sets illustration apart from fine art is that it is, by definition, commercial. Illustrators make art for a paying client, specifically to embellish something—a book, a magazine story, a journal cover, or even a website. Illustration is both an art form and a practical way to make an income. And related to illustration is licensing, when artists sell rights to a company to use their art on a product. The great thing about licensing is that it's a form of passive income; you can continue to earn royalties long after you've created the art. This chapter breaks down the worlds of illustration and licensing: what they are, how to find your place in the industry, and what to expect once you've landed your first gig.

WHAT IS ILLUSTRATION?

About two years into my art career, I got my first job. A publishing house contacted me about creating new artwork for a line of stationery. It hadn't occurred to me that I would ever be an illustrator. I'd always envisioned myself strictly as a fine artist, or someone who'd make and sell original works and archival prints. Once I started illustrating, however, I realized it was not only really enjoyable, but also a great way to add to my income. Since then, illustration has become my main source of income and my greatest passion.

Illustration is a unique art form that is defined not by its medium, but by its context. In many cases, being an illustrator requires both artistic and problem-solving skills. When you are hired for an illustration job, you typically work with an editor or an art director who gives you art direction, or a description of what they would like you to draw or paint. It often includes descriptive words, inspiration, reference imagery, and ideas to work with. Depending on the project, art direction may not always include concrete and detailed ideas because the art director may want to give you creative license to arrive at your own ideas or solutions.

If you have aspirations to become an illustrator, it's important to know the various illustration markets, which can range from personal clients and small companies to large corporations. A personal client is an individual who hires you to make an illustration like their blog header or a hand-drawn map for their wedding invitation. When you head into the commercial realm, most commonly your clients will belong to book, editorial, advertising, and retail product companies. In general, most illustrators will work in different markets during their career.

Personal Clients

If you've done fine art commissions for individuals and enjoy the satisfaction of making something festive or special, then producing illustrations for personal clients may be a great fit for you. Popular examples of this type of work include artwork and lettering for a wedding invitation, birth announcement, blog header, or small business logo. Personal client illustration work is different from commissioned fine art because the commissioning client has the ability to reproduce the art for his own purpose. If you are interested in getting personal clients, advertise your services through social media and your blog—and perhaps as a "custom" link in your shop. If you show examples of this kind of work in your portfolio, it won't be long before clients find you.

Book Illustration

Book illustration usually involves creating art for covers, jackets, or interior pages. Sometimes illustrations play a large role in a book, like in children's picture books, while other times illustrations are "spots" that play a supporting role highlighting information or a part of the story. Some illustrators make the majority of their living just doing book covers! The process of illustrating a book requires patience. It can often take a long time, not only to conceive and create, but also to hit the shelves. Because of the length of the printing process and long-term publication schedules, you might work on a book that does not appear in bookstores for more than a year. If you are interested in illustrating books, look for ones whose aesthetic fits yours and find the name of the publisher. Oftentimes, publishers have art submission guidelines on their website and you can send in pieces from your portfolio to introduce your work.

Editorial Illustration

Have you dreamed of seeing your art in the *New York Times* or the *Washington Post?* Editorial illustration is an exciting market that requires both quick thinking and quick turnaround. It encompasses creating artwork for magazines and newspapers to accompany a story or as the cover artwork. Creating illustrations for publications, especially for those that are published daily, is challenging and fast-paced with quick deadlines. This work demands great ideas, too, and often requires you to come up with the concepts—so art directors are looking for illustrators who can swiftly and adeptly think outside the box of literal images. If you are looking to get into editorial illustration, go to the websites or mastheads of your favorite magazines or newspapers and look for the names of art directors or senior designers. Email them samples of your work so that you can be considered for future editorial illustration assignments.

Advertising Illustration

The advertising market is a great place for illustrators who enjoy developing art that attracts customers to a product or service. Your client will most often be a large advertising or marketing firm that has been hired by a corporate client. This line of work typically pays well and lets you work with prestigious brands, but your name rarely accompanies the final work (as it would in a book or magazine). Often you are executing the vision of an advertising team that has settled on a strategy, and you may have less input into the concept as you might in other illustration markets. If you are interested in getting into the advertising market, taking out an ad in *Workbook* (see page 145) is a great way to put your name on an art buyer's radar. Send postcard mailings to art buyers or directors with images from your portfolio. Look at award annuals like *Communication Arts Illustration Annual* to get the names of art directors from various advertising agencies.

Greeting Card, Novelty, and Retail Product Illustration

Do you enjoy less conceptual, more decorative illustration work? Do you dream of having your artwork on journals, wallpaper, or fabric? Many illustrators spend their entire careers creating surface and pattern designs to adorn apparel, textiles, home décor, and paper products like stationery or greeting cards. Some of these jobs pay in flat fees, but many pay out in licensing royalties, which means if the product does well, you have the opportunity to earn quarterly checks based on the product's sales. If you are serious about breaking into this market, one point of entry is exhibiting at surface design trade shows like Printsource or Surtex. Retail product companies visit these trade shows to look for new talent. While taking out a booth can be expensive (thousands of dollars), you could pull together some illustrator friends to share a booth with you.

SUSIE GHAHREMANI

Painter and illustrator

SAN DIEGO, CALIFORNIA

WWW.BOYGIRLPARTY.COM

Susie Ghahremani was very single-minded in her pursuit to become an artist. "It didn't occur to me to do anything else. It was what I loved to do," she says. Susie began her career as a professional artist, landing her first shows and editorial illustration jobs while she was a student at Rhode Island School of Design (RISD). Combining her love of nature, music, and pattern, Susie paints her subject matters with a tiny brush and a steady hand. Her small-scale art requires intense concentration and precision and her work ethic is equally as focused. In addition to illustrating for commercial and editorial clients like Chronicle Books, Target, and the *New York Times*, she has her own stationery and gift line under her label, Boygirlparty. Susie also exhibits her paintings internationally and illustrated her first children's picture book, *What Will Hatch?* by Jennifer Ward, in 2013.

What were your first art-related jobs?

I had a really unusual crossover into the world of illustration because I started when I was still a student. I was into DIY and decided to draw my own stuff to sell. It just so happened that it was the perfect time to be doing this. It was the early 2000s, pre-Etsy, and the craft scene was just starting; people were discovering independent artist blogs and websites. I was at the forefront with an early Internet presence. Art directors were starting to look on the Internet as opposed to illustration annuals for illustrators. *BUST* magazine was one of my first big clients. They emailed me and hired me the next day. After that, I had more confidence to contact magazines and I sent postcards out. I sent one to *Martha Stewart Living* magazine and they hired me right away, too.

What illustration markets do you work in and do you have a favorite?

I work in almost every market, from editorial to stationery to publishing, and I have my own product line. And I love the variety, which means I don't have a favorite! You have to be open to changing gears if you are going to be a full-time artist. When you can diversify what you do, you are more likely to have income streams that will keep you busy. And you will never get bored.

You illustrated your first children's book, What Will Hatch? What was the process of illustrating a children's book like?

Every illustrator has an experience at least once in their career where one project takes up a big chunk of time. For me, this was a major project of two and a half years! When people see children's books they don't necessarily think that they take that long, but it is a massive process that involves the feedback of so many people. It was really challenging in a way that short-term projects are not. When you illustrate a book, it's the illustrator's responsibility to see through every single revision. I have done jobs with larger quantities of illustrations, but I have never sketched so many versions of something as when I illustrated this book. It was intense! It's a science-based book, so I got comments like "No, this kind of caterpillar would be on this kind of plant." So my illustrations couldn't be as imaginary as they usually are. And we had to make sure the illustrations could accompany versions that would be translated into other languages. I never imagined there could be that many new challenges for me in a project, but it goes to show you are never really settled even after thirteen years in the profession. It taught me a totally new way of working and I feel like that made it really worth all the effort.

Do you think going to art school gave you an advantage in that you started showing your work and doing illustration while you were still in school?

Yes, but that wasn't necessarily because of art school. Not everyone at art school showed their work. I was personally motivated to show my work. But there were other advantages to going to art school. There, you are surrounded by other people who are thinking differently—that made me more confident and gutsy to put my work out there and take risks. Also, the student-teacher relationships are priceless. All your teachers are working in the field and they are your inspiration. They are there to show you how to move forward. The advice from teachers was invaluable. I lucked out to have Jordin Isip as one of my teachers. He is a hardworking editorial illustrator. He was the one who guided me to the mastheads of my favorite magazines and showed me who to contact. I wouldn't have known how to pursue jobs if it wasn't for him.

How often do you do gallery shows?

It depends on what else I am doing. I get a lot of invitations from galleries and other artists curating shows. I do about one show per month, mostly group shows. I do only one solo show a year or every other year. For some group shows I make one or two pieces, while for others, I make up to sixteen or twenty pieces because my work is so small.

You've experienced some theft during gallery shows. How have you dealt with that?

That has been a learning process. I always have an open conversation with the galleries I work with. My work is miniature, so it has a greater tendency to be stolen than larger work. Land Gallery in Portland did the most amazing job. They glued everything down, and there were over two hundred paintings in that show, so it was a lot of work for them. It's devastating when your work is stolen. So I just try to communicate the importance of security measures and that the gallery is responsible if something happens to them. Most galleries have been extremely responsive. They don't want anything to be stolen, either.

FINDING YOUR NICHE

If you are a fine artist considering illustration, ask yourself, "Where do I see my work fitting best?" or "What kind of illustration market seems to be the most interesting to me?" When I was starting out I kept an inspiration board that depicted the kind of work I wanted to do and the illustration markets that seemed to resonate with me. Since my art is colorful and playful, but not always conceptual, I knew it would lend itself to products like stationery or home décor. I was also really interested in illustrating books, so I worked on making more narrative work for my portfolio. Taking the time to research where your work already fits, along with where you'd like to eventually land, will help inform which illustration markets to target and what adjustments to make to your work.

WHEN THE ART DIRECTOR CALLS

If you are new to illustration, you'll find the process is different than working with a gallery or even a client who requests a fine art commission. There are processes and expectations that the art director will assume you know, including using art direction, initiating and completing sketches, and rendering final artwork on deadline.

For most illustration jobs, the art director will contact you by email to see if you are interested and available for an assignment. Whether it's an editorial job, a book illustration gig, or a project creating artwork to adorn a product, the initial email and process are similar. Art directors will usually include a brief containing the core information for the project: a short description of what you need to illustrate, the number and size of the illustrations, the deadlines for rough artwork and final artwork, and, sometimes, the fee they will be extending to you. If you are interested in the project and can meet the project's deadlines, make sure to ask the art director any questions that weren't addressed in the brief to gauge your ability to complete the job properly (for example, how many sketches would they like?). It's good etiquette to respond to these emails quickly and with a great degree of professionalism, even if it's a job you can't take. Building positive relationships with potential clients is part of what will keep a steady stream of work rolling in.

NEGOTIATING YOUR FEE

Part of being a successful illustrator is getting fair compensation for the work you do. Comfortably discussing fees is a regular part of doing work as an illustrator. It helps to look at negotiation as a game in which everyone is a winner (including the client). And it gets easier the more you do it. If you are working on your own and without an illustration agency, it's important to become familiar with the industry standards for pricing different types of illustration work. *The Graphic Artists Guild Handbook: Pricing & Ethical Guidelines* is a great resource for this.

Before negotiating, you need to get all the information you can about the specifics of the job because it will be the basis for establishing what you should be paid. If an art director asks for your fee, don't feel obliged to give a spur-of-the-moment price that you may later regret. Once you've stated your fee, it will be harder to argue for a greater amount. Instead, it sometimes helps to respond by asking, "What is your budget?" This way, you won't be throwing out a number without knowing if it is even in the ballpark. Some clients, like magazine and book publishers, will tell you up front what their budget is for a particular job. Sometimes this fee is set in stone because it's all they've budgeted, but many times clients will quote a fee expecting that you might negotiate for more.

Plan ahead and think critically about the compensation you'd like for a job and why you think it's warranted. Make sure your fee accounts for anything that makes the job more challenging or unique, and think broadly about all aspects of the job, including the rights to the imagery, the level of work involved in rendering the illustrations, the size of the illustration, and the turnaround time. For example, you can tell a client, "For a three-day turnaround my fee is $2,000, but with a seven-day turnaround, my fee is $1,500." This way, you are negotiating not only the fee, but also the time you need to complete the project. If the client fee is set in stone and it's a job you'd like to take but think the amount is too low, you can also say, "Let's take a look at how it can be done for that price," which might include extending the deadline or reducing the work involved.

ILLUSTRATION CONTRACTS

Once you have negotiated a fee, a contract will outline your agreements. You want to make sure that all the terms you agreed to over the phone or email are included in writing. Often, the client will provide the contract, but be prepared to make one in case they do not. (*The Graphic Artists Guild Handbook: Pricing & Ethical Guidelines* has samples of illustration contracts that you can use.) Reading the contract carefully before you sign it is critical. This might be difficult because contracts are written using legalese that can seem confusing or intimidating. I cannot stress enough how important it is to understand the meaning of everything in the contract before signing, even if it means taking time and getting help to translate it. If you don't have an agent, you can hire a lawyer at an hourly rate to review your contract. Search for a lawyer in your community who specializes in contract law. Some communities also have nonprofit organizations that specialize in helping artists with legal issues and may have recommendations for legal help. Below are some of the things an illustration contract could include:

Project specifics: Details about what you'll be delivering including the number of illustrations and the expected rounds of modifications, the size, medium, and intended use.

Terms of payment: How much will be paid for an illustration, when payment is due, and the penalties for not paying it on time. Sometimes with large illustration jobs the contract will divide the job into installments that are paid incrementally. This is helpful for jobs that will take a long time so you don't have to wait until the end of the job to receive the entire amount.

Rights: Who owns the rights to the illustration, for how long, and in what geographic regions. By default, without a contract, artists own both the copyright and the reproduction rights for each piece of work for seventy-five years from the time the work was created. This means that no one can reproduce your work without your permission. However, when you sign an illustration contract, you are selling the client the right to reproduce your work in a very specific way and for a limited amount of time.

Credit: How you will be credited in the book, magazine, or product line. If this is important to you, make sure there is a line in the contract stating how you want to your name or business name to appear.

Kill fee: The amount (or percentage of the total amount) due to an artist if the client pulls the plug on the job or does not accept your work. For example, if an editorial client rejects the work you've produced, their kill fee might be 25 percent. If you create the contract yourself, you could specify a kill fee on your contract commensurate with the amount of work you've done.

Work-for-hire: A clause that sometimes appears in a contract that means that the author of the work is credited to the client and the copyright also belongs to them as well. Work-for-hire is less common but does occur more legitimately when illustrators make art for company identities (e.g., a logo) or very specific company advertising. Look out for this clause and make sure it's warranted before signing on the dotted line, since some companies may attempt to get artists to sign away more rights than are necessary.

Promoting yourself as an illustrator requires using all of the techniques covered in chapter 3, including a strong website, social media, print promotions, and person-to-person networking. But there are some additional outlets specifically for illustrators that can further promote your work to art buyers and directors.

American Illustration. *American Illustration* is a yearly, juried illustration annual. Nabbing a spot in *American Illustration* is the height of prestige in the illustration industry. It is a competition, so only illustrators chosen by a panel of distinguished jurors are included in each year's edition. Artists can submit images at about $50 per image. More than seven thousand images are submitted each year by more than a thousand illustrators, and an average of three hundred illustrators are chosen each year for the annual. The annual has a readership of thirty thousand, including many art directors from the world's most prestigious agencies and companies.

Society of Illustrators Annual Exhibition. This juried exhibition sponsored by the Society of Illustrators showcases some of the most outstanding works created each year. The competition is open to artists worldwide and judged by a jury of professionals, which include renowned illustrators, art directors, and designers. All winning entries are published in the *Illustrators Annual Book* and the original work exhibited at the Museum of American Illustration at the Society of Illustrators. Entry fees are generally under $100.

Communication Arts Illustration Annual. As with *American Illustration*, a jury of distinguished designers, art directors, and illustrators select the artists to be featured in the annual. The competition is stiff, with thousands of entries for only a few hundred spots. For a fee of less than $100 for a series of illustrations, artists can enter a variety of categories like books, advertising, and editorial. The winning entries are showcased in the yearly publication and on their website, providing great exposure to chosen illustrators.

Work/Life. First published by Uppercase Publishing in 2010, *Work/Life* is a juried publication that comes out every two years and features a hundred international illustrators, each with a full spread showcasing samples of their work, client list, and images of their workspaces. It has become a celebrated resource for art buyers looking for talented illustrators. Inclusion in *Work/Life* is more affordable for artists than *Workbook* (the submission fee ranges from $400 to $600).

Workbook. *Workbook* is a publication published twice a year in which illustrators or illustration agencies can take out advertisements. Ads are offered at full page or full spread, and you must design your own ad according to their specifications. They also have a website with a directory that features online portfolios for illustrators. *Workbook* is distributed worldwide to major buyers at advertising agencies, design studios, publications, and Fortune 500 companies. Advertisements can be pricey, ranging from $800 to more than $3,000, depending on which options you choose for size, digital distribution, and marketing services.

EXECUTING THE ASSIGNMENT

Once you've accepted a job and the contract is signed, the art director or editor will likely send you art direction, often with suggested color palettes, reference images, and specific details to guide your work. Read it carefully to make sure you understand what the client is looking for. Don't be afraid to ask for additional information to get a full picture of your artistic task; this will save you time and effort later on. Art directors usually appreciate illustrators who dig deeply into a project and want to get the artwork just right. Once you have the information you need, you can begin sketching. Most illustrators complete sketches, sometimes called "roughs," in pencil, ink, or digital format in a simplistic form. You will be providing a general outline or simple illustration typically without much elaboration. Depending on the job, clients may ask for only one sketch to upwards of five different versions so they can choose the one they like the best. The sketching phase is often the longest, because the client offers feedback to improve the sketch until it's ready to go to final artwork; this generally takes about two to three rounds of changes.

Make sure your sketch is fully approved in writing before moving on to final artwork. Use the approved sketch as the basis for your final artwork, from dimensions and scale to the details of how individual elements are rendered. While the sketch is just a rough basis for the final artwork, the client usually expects to see finished artwork that looks just like it, except in final color and often with more detail. It should be as clean and beautiful as possible. Sometimes art directors will ask for changes to a piece of final artwork after you've submitted it, but the goal is to keep those changes minimal by getting the final artwork as close to the approved sketch as possible.

If you find yourself in a situation where you cannot meet a project deadline, be sure to email the art director immediately to explain the situation and ask for an extension. Often, if you are proactive and forthright, art directors will work with you to adjust the schedule.

 ## DO YOUR BEST WORK

When you begin to get several illustration assignments at a time, you might be tempted to treat some jobs as more important than others—perhaps because you like one client more or are more excited about a book cover than a small spot illustration for a magazine. While prioritizing your work is normal, it's crucial that you do your best work for every job regardless of how small it is. Sometimes the smallest, most seemingly insignificant jobs lead to bigger and more exciting opportunities. Treat every job like it is important to your future because you never know where it might lead.

BILLING YOUR CLIENTS

When the job is finished, it's time to bill the client. You will need to create an invoice to inform the client that payment is due and what the payment terms are. Typical payment terms are "net thirty," which means that the client has thirty days to pay from the date on the invoice. It's also common to charge late fees if payment is past due; just be sure to note that policy on your invoice. Remember that oral requests do not take the place of invoices! In most cases, a client cannot pay artists unless an invoice has been submitted because their accounting department requires it. It is a good practice to deliver your invoice with the final artwork or immediately after it's been accepted. You can also withhold the client's right to use your work until the payment has been received, but this should be spelled out in your contract.

THE WORLD OF ART LICENSING

"Licensing" is the term used to describe the agreement that takes place when you sell the right to a company to use your art on their products. It is a growing industry for artists to feature their art on a variety of products like textiles, home décor, children's games, and stationery. The best part of this income stream is that it is often passive, which means that you are earning income with very little effort. "It has been awesome part-time income," notes artist Alyson Fox. "Here I was, not doing any of the labor, yet making money from my work. I love collaborations because you share the work with another person or set of people." Often, companies will contact you to purchase the rights to an existing artwork in your portfolio; they place the artwork on their product and then you earn royalties whenever that product is sold. It can be easy money and some illustrators have been known to make their entire income from licensing royalties alone. Licensing gigs that require you to make new artwork for a client often pay more money since additional work and time are required.

If you are interested in breaking into licensing, there are many things you can do to increase the chances your work will be picked up. Typically, companies who license art are looking for themes that they can use across a range of products, like a set of stationery products or a line of textiles. They are looking for groupings of similar artwork that are a part of a collection. So it's important to create your work in sets. If you can offer sets of four or five pieces of art in a themed collection, companies are more able to make more products with it. Repeat patterns are also attractive to companies. You may want to learn to turn your art into repeat patterns using programs like Photoshop or Illustrator. And if you create sets of complementary patterns, that is even more beneficial.

You should also consider visiting and eventually exhibiting in one of the licensing shows like Surtex or Printsource in New York. Visiting will give you an idea of what the licensing market looks like and the kinds of artwork that artists are selling to different markets like apparel, home décor, or fabric. You want your artwork to be unique and fresh and seeing what is currently on the market will help you think more critically about how to make your work stand out.

Last, contact your dream companies! Some companies even provide submission guidelines on their site. When they don't, attempt to find the address or email for the art buyer or art director at the company. When you contact them, show them artwork that is in line with what they already offer but is different enough in style or subject matter that it will be new and interesting for them.

Once you get a licensing deal, it might be tempting to envision your artwork on every product under the sun. But for some artists there are downsides to licensing. Do you want your work to be perceived as overly commercial? Do you want your artwork on products that may not fit with your own aesthetic? Being selective about where you license your work will help prevent any regrets down the road. Work only with companies whose products you admire and ask to see product samples to inspect the quality. Talk to fellow artists who license with the company and ask about their own experience—if they are pleased with working with the company, their products, and the royalty income. Better to have your art on a few items that you are really proud of rather than on a mishmash of products you'd rather hide in your closet.

LICENSING CONTRACTS

When you license your work to a company, you're agreeing to give them certain rights for use. Since licensing deals can be very detailed, it's critical to understand the contract to protect yourself and the company you are working with from any legal disputes down the road. Licensing contracts typically contain terms that describe the artwork, rights to it, exclusivity, duration, territory, and payment. When you develop art for a licensed product, the contract could also include deadlines and details on how the work should be delivered. Here are some terms you might see in a licensing contract:

Grant of license: Establishes the agreement between the company and artist and states which pieces of artwork the company is licensing and on which products the company has the rights to use them.

Exclusivity: Normally delineates artwork or products to which the company has exclusive rights. Sometimes companies request exclusive rights to use your work on a particular product or set of products. For example, you may sell a repeat pattern to a company for use on a journal and wrapping paper. The contract may stipulate that no other company can use any of your artwork on wrapping paper or any other paper product. Some companies may simply request exclusivity only on that specific artwork, so you cannot self-publish or license it anywhere else for any purpose. Other companies may not be concerned with exclusivity at all. The thing to look out for most is whether a company wants exclusivity to you. A stationery company might try to stipulate that you cannot work with any other stationery company, even for different products or with different designs. Exclusivity, in most cases, comes with a price; the more definitive the buyout of your work, the higher the royalty fee, so if you do give exclusivity, charge for it. Sometimes you can negotiate a term to the exclusivity, which gives the company confidence their product won't be cannibalized by something competitive and also gives you the ultimate right to leverage your illustration in new ways after a few years.

Duration: How long a company will have rights to your art. Like exclusivity, duration can often drive up the price—if the company wants lifetime rights, then the fees for your work will be higher. Sometimes duration will stipulate "lifetime of the product," which often makes more sense for the artist than simple lifetime rights because if the product stops selling, the rights are then granted back to the artist.

Territory: Rights to your art within a certain geographic region. At times companies want worldwide rights to your work; other times it's limited to a smaller region. For example, if you have an exclusive contract stipulating worldwide rights with a certain American quilt fabric company, it means that you cannot enter into a contract with another quilt fabric company in any country.

Royalties: Your earnings that are a percentage of the sale of the product featuring your art. Royalties are typically paid quarterly. Your royalty could be 5 percent of the suggested retail price of the product, which may sound low, but if the company estimates millions of dollars in sales, it adds up quickly.

Advance: The amount of money you are paid initially when you agree to license your work. It's usually an "advance against royalties," or an advance payment against your future earnings. You'd begin receiving royalty checks once the product has earned out the amount of the advance. Not all companies pay advances, but you can negotiate with the company to include one, especially if you are creating new work that requires time and effort up front.

Flat fee: A flat amount for your artwork (instead of royalties) when you agree to license it. In some cases, this can be a good thing—especially if you are paid up front. But if the product has potential to do well, royalties are often a smarter way to go, since you are earning a percentage of the sale of the product.

Before signing a licensing contract, take the time to negotiate for fees and rights that you feel comfortable with. It's perfectly acceptable to ask for sales projections and estimates based on past sales of similar products before making a decision. If the company is new or fails to give you this information, think twice before signing. If they can give you this information, look at whether the projected royalties are going to be worth limiting a piece of your art to this product. If the licensee is really excited about your work and you have some leverage, you can request a "guaranteed minimum annual royalty payment," where the licensee promises to pay you a specific amount, usually at the beginning of every year, regardless of how well the merchandise sells during the year. At the end of that year, if the earned royalties exceed that amount, then you're paid the difference.

ILLUSTRATION AND LICENSING AGENTS

One of the most common questions I field from illustrators emerging from school or attempting to expand their careers is, "Should I sign with an illustration agent?" As with many things in the world of the professional artist, the answer depends on your goals, skill set, and preferences. While having an agent can change your freelance career, many illustrators prefer to handle their own contracts and client relationships.

Having an agent has many benefits. For one, they can make connections with big-name clients that you might not be able to make on your own. They can also secure more lucrative deals for you since they negotiate your contracts. Often, having an agent lends cachet in the eyes of art directors. Art directors may be more likely to hire agented illustrators, since they assume these artists come with a level of experience or professionalism. Though you'll be giving away a chunk of your pay (usually about 25 to 45 percent of the payment you receive from a job), the trade-off is having someone who handles your contracts, bills and collects payment from clients, and finds you new work. Agencies also work hard to promote their artists through social networking, blogging, industry lookbooks, magazines, trade shows, and promotional mailings.

Illustration agents also have knowledge of the industry standards for what artists should be paid for certain types of jobs or licensing deals. This relieves the worry "Should I ask for more money?" that many illustrators have when a client offers them a fee for a project. In addition, they review your contracts and manage all the back-and-forth with clients, negotiating the terms of the agreement. This saves time and stress and can be advantageous for busy illustrators who don't have time to delve into the minutiae of a contract.

Another advantage to having an agent is that they can intervene if you ever have difficulty with a client. I often tell friends that I've never had to have any uncomfortable conversations with clients because my agency handles them for me! I once worked on a job where the client asked for what seemed like endless rounds of changes—even changing things back to what they'd been in a previous round. When we were up to seven rounds of changes, things began to feel unfair and rotten. Instead of having to address the issue directly with my client, I simply called my agent, who handled the entire situation for me.

Great agents take on multiple roles, acting as mentors, coaches, bookkeepers, bill collectors, expert communicators, and useful resources, all in one package. It's important to remember that your agent works for you—they are there to support and guide you (and do a lot of hard work on your behalf). But they are also depending on you to uphold your end of the relationship. When you have an agent, you are expected to work hard, continually add new work to your portfolio, act in a professional manner, and communicate promptly and effectively, both with the agency and clients.

BETSY CORDES

Licensing consultant and
creative manager

SAN FRANCISCO, CALIFORNIA

WWW.FEBRUARY13CREATIVE.COM

Betsy Cordes's extensive experience in the field of commercial art includes product design, art direction, management of creative teams, and loads of art licensing deals—including negotiations from both sides of the table. As an art director, she has helped companies like Cardstore.com, Papyrus, and Madison Park Greetings find and license the work of scores of talented artists. As an artist herself, she has licensed her own work for greeting cards, gift packaging, and other products. As a creative manager and advisor, she works with artists on brand development, licensing, and business management.

The art licensing market is full with the work of so many artists. What advice do you have for artists to find their own voice in such a large industry?

Ask yourself, What am I really about as an artist? What comes naturally to me? What do I lose myself in? Many inexperienced artists start mimicking what they see instead of developing their own point of view. It's okay to be inspired, and looking at the work of other artists is a great way to learn, but it's not okay to copy the work or distinct style of other artists and sell it as your own. The ultimate aim of any artist, even commercial artists, is to do what is uniquely you. Take the time to develop your own unique style. On a practical level, this means not trying to break into licensing as the first step in your career while you are still figuring out your style. Selling your work directly to customers will give you an opportunity to learn what pieces of your work sell, and that will help you when you go in search of licensing opportunities.

How do companies find new artists?

Art directors mostly find new artists online through their websites, shops, blogs, and social media. Traditional methods like taking out an expensive ad or doing a huge postcard mailing are still useful, but more so when coupled with a strong web presence. Art directors might stumble on your work on Pinterest or Tumblr, so anything you can do to ensure your name is on it, whether it's a small signature or copyright at the bottom of the image, will help them find you. Trade shows, like Surtex, are another great way to get in front of art directors. They are not cheap, so save your money for a booth when you know you are ready for that step. Art and craft fairs like Renegade are another place art directors look for new talent.

Also, when you are out in the world shopping for yourself, pay attention to products that have artwork on them. Home in on products and manufacturers that seem like the best fit for you and your aesthetic. Once you have a list of companies you'd be interested in working with, go on their websites to see if they have artist submission guidelines. If they don't, you can be bold and make a phone call to the company. Politely ask if there is someone in product development who makes art buying or licensing decisions and request their contact information. Then make your pitch to the correct person, as briefly and professionally as possible. Ask if they take submissions and the best way to get your work in front of them. If you get an email address for someone, attach no more than five low-resolution images—72 dpi and approximately 5 x 6 inches. Obviously, include a link to your website or another place they can see your work.

What should artists look out for when negotiating licensing contracts?

You want to make sure the rights you are granting for use of your artwork are clearly and narrowly defined. You own the copyright to your work, and a licensing contract means you are essentially leasing the work to a company for a specific purpose and for a specific amount of time. Get help understanding your first contract, or even your first few, until you are well versed in licensing contract language. I recommend hiring a lawyer or someone with licensing experience. The first thing you want to be sure of is that it's a licensing contract and not a work-for-hire contract. When you sign a work-for-hire agreement, it means that you are agreeing to complete that work for the company as if you are an employee, and you will not own it. That means they can do whatever they want with your work, without your permission or consent.

The *Graphic Artists Guild Handbook: Pricing & Ethical Guidelines* is the bible for understanding contracts and an indispensible resource for people getting into licensing or illustration. It does a great job of explaining what copyright is all about, including some of these finer points like "buyout," "all rights," or "work-for-hire" and the differences between those terms. We tend to refer to copyright as one thing, but it's actually a bundle of rights—your right to display the work, reproduce the work, make money from the work, and create derivative work.

Be wary of exclusivity. One key to making good money in licensing is to have the same individual piece of art on multiple products. The way to effectively do that is to narrowly define the usage that you grant for each agreement that you sign. Exclusivity can also extend to you as an artist. Bolt fabric is the only market where exclusivity to one company is standard, but in every other market, it's not. So watch out for that.

Are there situations where licensing deals can work against an artist?

There are ways that jobs can work against artists. For example, let's say you get a great corporate branding job where your illustrations are used all over product packaging. Your style comes to represent that brand in the eyes of consumers. Someone who might otherwise love to decorate their home with your prints and pillows might see your work and can't help but think of the brand. It's important to think about what can potentially happen down the road as you contemplate licensing deals.

As much as you want to make smart business decisions, you also want to stay true to your values and aesthetics. Ask for samples of products from the companies you might work with before signing an agreement. Make sure they are of a quality you can stand by. Ask to see a production sample before they go into full production. Stipulate that the sample has to be approved by you before going into production.

How should artists present final artwork to a licensee?

All companies want professionally executed artwork. In the simplest terms, this means it's important to understand the different production design terms—like the difference between CMYK and RGB and what bleed, trim size, and resolution mean. When you work with a licensee, you should prepare your artwork in a format that is easy for them to work with. For example, a journal cover might have a full painting on it of, say, a rich floral motif with birds and bees. But the manufacturer might also want to put spot art of the birds and bees on the back of the journal. If you submit artwork that has all the elements layered, the manufacturer can lift these elements and use them in different ways.

What are the three most important things artists should remember as they pursue art licensing?

1) Remember that it takes time to earn money from licensing, so you want to diversify your income by selling your work in other ways. 2) Learn how to digitally manipulate and extend your artwork so that you can leverage each piece for as many opportunities as you can find. Having collections of flexible, versatile artwork comes in handy. 3) Don't be afraid to ask questions—of your lawyer, the company, your agent or consultant. You are not going to lose the deal because you ask a lot of questions. In the end, asking questions shows you are smart and take your work seriously.

FINDING AN AGENT

Every agency is different—from the look and feel of their artist roster to the kinds of work their artists do. While many agencies represent a wide range of artists, some agencies specialize in amassing artists whose work lends itself to licensing or editorial illustration. Many agencies choose to work only with more experienced and already-successful artists, and other agencies keep an eye toward new artists who might become the next big name. Some agencies prefer to be small and exclusive and may keep their roster to no more than ten to thirty artists. Others are larger, representing hundreds of artists, and constantly seeking out new talent. While some agencies do not take submissions and prefer to seek out their own talent, others do take submissions and review them regularly.

If you are interested in finding an illustration agent, the most important thing to remember is that they look for artists who create work that is marketable and will sell in one or more of the illustration markets. They also usually look for artists who have a strong individual style. You want to be represented by an agent who values your style and is excited to promote your work, so find an agent who is a good fit aesthetically. You can begin your search by finding artists with an aesthetic similar to yours or whose work you like and find out if they have an agent. (Usually, if an illustrator has an agent, the agent's name is listed on their website.) Check out that agent's roster of artists and the work they do to consider whether your work fits in, but is distinctive enough that it won't get lost. Also look at their list of clients to see if they are clients that you'd like to work with and would be tough get on your own. Learn as much as you can about an agency's operation: How long have they been around? How big are they? How many artists do they represent? Do they have a staff of people to work with their artists?

Once you've narrowed your list of potential agencies, always contact them one at a time, starting with your first choice. Find out if the agency has a submission process by looking on their website. If they don't, you can inquire via email to find out how to send your work. If you know of an artist who works with the agency already, ask if they'd be gracious enough to write an introductory email. It's important to remember that some agencies are so popular that they receive thousands of submissions a year! It may take weeks or months for them to write back. If the agency does express interest, be prompt and professional in your response. If possible, set up an in-person meeting to share your portfolio. In-person meetings also give you an opportunity to see if you have rapport with the agent.

If an agent is interested in signing you, they will extend a contract that will cover, at minimum, the agency's expectations for its artists, the commission rate, the length of the contract, and how to end the relationship if it doesn't work out. Most agencies will require that they handle all of your contracts, even if the job did not come through them and the client contacted you directly. If you are a more experienced artist, it may be possible to retain a list of existing clients that you work with outside your agency. Read your contract carefully for things such as yearly fees and what your obligations are to the agency in return for their services.

WORKING WITHOUT AN AGENT

Having an illustration agent can be beneficial in many ways, but having an agent is not essential to a successful illustration career. It used to be that in order to get your work in front of art directors, signing with an agent was essential. Now, with social media platforms and online venues for sharing your portfolio, marketing your own work to art directors is easy and low-cost. Having an agent is not necessarily for everyone, and being represented by an agency does not guarantee that you will get a steady stream of work. In fact, many illustrators prefer working on their own and managing their own work.

The most significant benefit to working on your own is financial. When you work on your own, you do 100 percent of the work and you get 100 percent of the illustration fee. For some artists, the occasional strife that comes with handling their own work is worth not handing over the commission you would otherwise pay an agent. For jobs that pay upwards of $10,000 or more (and there are illustration jobs that do), having an agent would mean paying thousands of dollars to someone else. Many agencies also charge fees for yearly promotion that may or may not benefit you. Without an agency, you can invest your money in promotion that works best for your own individual needs and niche in the market.

Most agents have the best interests of their illustrators at heart and are highly professional, but as middlemen, they may inadvertently get in the way of your ability to build a positive working relationship with an art director or art buyer. Since artists are sometimes left out of discussions regarding potential projects or licensing deals early on in the negotiations, it can be hard to know if your agent is representing you and your interests fully. Additionally, any of your agent's words or actions, especially any that the client perceives negatively, may reflect poorly on you. When you work on your own, you have more control over communication with clients. If you are just starting out as an illustrator, the experience you gain in developing your own client relationships and negotiating contracts with art directors will be valuable—regardless of whether you choose eventually to work with an agent or not.

Another benefit to working without an agent is the freedom to accept or decline jobs that come your way. While many agencies protect their artists from overwork or taking jobs that don't seem right, some agents may pressure you to take every opportunity that comes your way. When you work on your own, you get to decide what work you take on, without apology or explanation.

While many illustrators work on their own negotiating contracts, sending invoices, promoting their work, and managing client relationships, many also hire help on occasion. For example, it's good to find a lawyer you can reach out to review contracts when necessary. You might also consider hiring an assistant to manage things like billing clients, promoting your work, or building an archive of your illustration work. (See "Hiring Help" in chapter 7 for more information.)

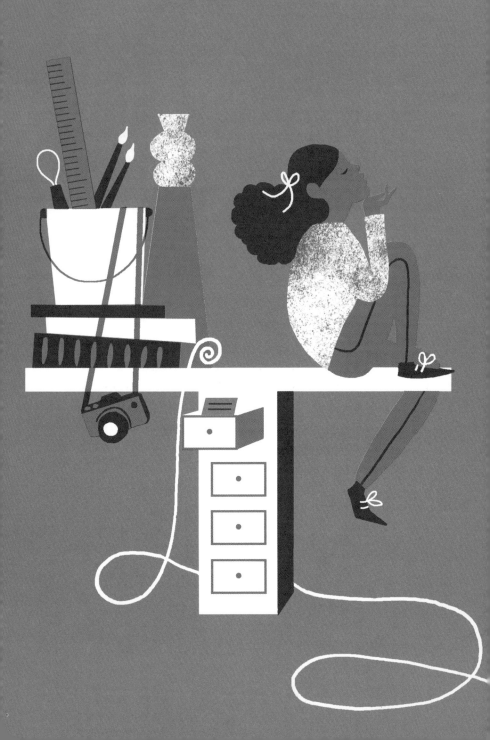

MANAGING THE EBB *and* FLOW OF SUCCESS

Perhaps the most exciting aspect of being a full-time working artist is the limitless potential for success. Once you shed the notion that an artist's life is made of struggle, you open yourself up to endless possibilities for exploration, innovation, and growth. The potential can be so great that many artists who originally thought they might struggle find themselves with more opportunities than they can comfortably handle. In every artist's career, there will be ups: work is flowing to you, clients are emailing with new projects, your work is selling; and inevitably some downs: no new opportunities are coming your way, sales are slow, money is tight. The advice in this chapter is meant to help you learn how to manage your career at both ends of this spectrum. You'll see that either situation is rife with challenges but presents opportunities to change, build, and grow.

MAKING THE MOST OF DOWNTIME

A freelance artist's career can be unpredictable. But even when times are slow, it is still full of potential for organization, learning, and growth. When you're going through a slower period, it's critical to maintain regular work hours and stay engaged in the development of your art business with the following activities:

.... *Build your portfolio.* One of the best ways to use downtime is to build your portfolio by working on personal work. You might start making artwork that you could envision on actual products like journal covers, tea towels, or children's flash cards. This will add a body of work to your portfolio that makes it easy for potential clients to see how they could adapt your work for their line. You could also approach a local gallery to try to schedule a show featuring your new work.

.... *Volunteer.* Chapter 4 covered the importance of getting involved in your local arts community as a way to network and make connections that will benefit your future as an artist. Consider using your downtime to volunteer at an arts nonprofit or arts space, or intern or work part-time at a gallery. At a gallery you'll learn about how galleries sell art to collectors, what's involved in putting together and installing exhibitions, and how artists and gallery owners work together. When you volunteer at an arts nonprofit, you can learn about applying for grants, opportunities to show your work in exhibition programs, and participating in large art fundraisers like auctions.

.... *Work on marketing.* Use downtime to get your name out there as much as you can. Review your marketing materials: Is your website up to date? If not, take the time to add any new pieces, press, or awards, and even improve the look and feel of it. Have you been keeping up with social media? Spend time interacting on Facebook, Twitter, and Instagram, and explore different ways to leverage it. Have you posted on your blog lately? Start a personal project that you can post about on it. Have you recently sent a postcard mailing to your dream galleries or list of art directors? Use this time to create a new postcard featuring your favorite new work.

TEACHING

As you move through your career, you are constantly growing as an artist, even in ways that may not seem obvious. As you labor diligently toward deadlines, your artwork shifts and improves on a daily basis. As you experience new opportunities, you gain confidence and perspective. For many, teaching is a way to grow as an artist and a natural extension of the art-making process. Teaching increases your visibility and establishes you as a leader in your medium as you share your talents and techniques with an eager audience. It also forces you to step outside of your process and explain it to others. You may find yourself saying, "I never realized I did it this way!" Many artists run regular classes out of their studios or produce e-courses online providing instruction through video and written materials. Some artists with graduate degrees even teach full- or part-time at the collegiate level.

For some artists, teaching is such a meaningful extension of their practice that it becomes a main source of income. A single workshop can net several hundred dollars to more than a thousand dollars, depending on fees and number of participants. Having a successful online course can bring as much as several thousand dollars since there is often no limit to the number of people who can sign up.

Wondering if teaching is right for you? Give it a try! Do you enjoy working with children or is your work or your technique a good fit for kids? If so, teaching children might be a good place to start. If you prefer to interact with adults or your process is advanced, then instructing grown-ups is more likely a better fit for you. Start by finding a gallery, organization, or business in your community that hosts art classes. Often these organizations manage marketing, enrollment, and scheduling, so you can focus on developing the curriculum for your class. Some of these organizations gladly accept proposals for classes and will work with you to tailor your class to just the right people in their existing audience.

Another option is to try online teaching. There are many businesses that host online classes and continually accept proposals for classes to add to their offerings. These businesses help you market your class, take care of sign-ups and scheduling, give you tips on developing a curriculum, and teach you the basics of using video to share your process (a must in online art instruction).

ARTIST RESIDENCIES

Artist residencies offer great opportunities for artists to grow, since they provide dedicated time and space for creative work. "It's inspiring to create alongside other hardworking artists, and the time and space can often yield an opportunity for rapid growth," notes artist Shannon Rankin, who has participated in several residencies. Some support one artistic genre, but many are interdisciplinary and include artists such as writers or actors. There are programs where members of the public interact with your work and others that offer more solitude.

Many residencies provide room and board and offer an opportunity for artists to work alongside each other, providing separate studio spaces under one roof. Location, living arrangements, duration, and workspace environments are all important factors to consider before applying for a residency. For Shannon Rankin, residencies that provide ample space are key. "Access to a large studio gives me the opportunity to explore larger work or installations, which I can't do at my home studio." Fortunately, there are plenty of different types of residencies (see Resources). Depending on your needs, there are month-long residencies in the countryside or week-long experiences in large cities.

Some residences are highly competitive with specific prerequisites and applicants are selected through a juried process. Others accept all applicants depending on space availability. Most residencies simply require that you enjoy the environment and work on your practice without any specific expectations about what you accomplish while you are there. Others may require you to show the work you made in an exhibition at the end of your residency. While residencies are fantastic opportunities, they are also a commitment. Leaving your studio and life—especially for longer residencies far from home—requires making plans to manage aspects of your art business, like paying your bills and attending to email, while you are away. Take the time to consider the impact of a residency on your life and art practice before you commit.

MANAGING A BUSY WORKLOAD

Many artists go through periods when they say yes to too many jobs with overlapping deadlines. Prime example: I said yes to five big illustration jobs at the same time that I was planning my wedding. I was exhausted, burned out, and could barely enjoy the process of planning my big day. After it was over, I wondered how I could have let that happen. I was doing the work I loved, and yet, because there was so much of it, I felt anxious and exhausted. Fortunately, when we go through busy periods, we are forced to take stock of our choices and habits. Often busy times lead us to create new and healthier habits like taking on fewer projects at once, getting organized, or taking better care of ourselves by making time for exercise or rest.

Getting organized will help alleviate much of the stress of a busy schedule. I was formerly a project manager and I began to apply the same organizational techniques to my workload as an artist. I started with spreadsheets that listed all my projects and their deadlines. I would visit it daily and keep it updated. Since then, I've also begun keeping a large chart of my current projects. It helps me to stay on top of all the moving parts and to reassure me that I haven't forgotten anything. My chart is on my office wall and is an ever-present large visual for me. As I accomplish things, I mark them off, giving me a sense of satisfaction.

It's also helpful to make a daily detailed to-do list and think about your workload in smaller chunks so that it doesn't feel so overwhelming. Other artists prefer to use online task managers like Google Task or Todoist to manage their projects. Many online task managers allow you to group specific tasks under larger project headings, and to prioritize both projects and the smaller associated tasks, allowing you to see the most important tasks at a glance. Other artists use calendars as the basis for their project management. "I make a lot of lists," says artist Michelle Armas. "And then I transfer everything to the calendar so I can visualize how much time there is for each task." Understanding how projects might overlap is something a calendar can help you do. This is important information, not only when planning your work flow, but also to gauge if you have the bandwidth to take on new work opportunities.

 ## KEEP IT STOCKED

As an artist, your work inherently requires a lot of supplies, from art supplies like paint and brushes to shipping supplies like envelopes, boxes, and bubble wrap. Because we are so dependent on material goods, nothing is quite as frustrating as being on a roll with a project only to discover you've run out of paint or another important material. Suddenly, your project stops dead in its tracks. Since last-minute trips for supplies waste valuable time and can throw off your work flow, take one day a month to inventory important supplies and then spend the rest of the day shopping for them. During especially busy times like the preholiday season, check your supplies weekly and replenish them quickly.

FLORA BOWLEY

Painter

PORTLAND, OREGON

WWW.BRAVEINTUITIVEYOU.COM

Artist Flora Bowley's first show was at a local coffee shop when she was still in college. While selling her first paintings at that show, she had a lightbulb moment: she realized that she could someday make a living as an artist. All her actions from that point forward were in service of meeting this goal. Eventually, Flora became a successful studio artist known for her large-scale, multilayered abstract works. Later, she discovered teaching as another creative outlet and income source. Her painting workshops, held in locations worldwide and also as e-courses, have become one of her greatest passions, introducing enthusiastic beginners to her technique. In 2012, Flora added another feather to her cap by sharing her holistic and empowering approach to painting in her first book, *Brave Intuitive Painting*.

You started your art business years ago when you were still in college. What steps did you take after school to make art your full-time career?

I developed this strategy that I had to somehow make fifty dollars an hour at whatever I did outside of making art, so that I had to work only ten hours a week or less. That way, I could spend the majority of my time painting. So I waitressed at fancy restaurants, became a yoga teacher, and even a massage therapist. I pieced all of those jobs together until I got to the point when I didn't have to do them anymore and I could earn a full-time living from my art. It didn't happen overnight.

What are some of the different ways that you make your income?

I sell original paintings, mostly through a handful of galleries that carry my work. Occasionally, I do specific commissions for individuals or businesses as well. I also sell some original paintings as prints through my website. I've also licensed my work to companies.

And of course, I make a big portion of my income from teaching. I teach a painting e-course that I run three times a year called "Bloom True." And I teach in-person painting workshops around the world. When I started teaching a few years ago, I said yes to pretty much everything, so I found myself flying around the world teaching weekend workshops, which became pretty exhausting. Now, I teach about four week-long workshops in faraway places like Bali, Mexico, and Europe, along with about five shorter (three- to four-day) workshops in the United States.

How do you set up the locations and find students for the classes?

When I first started teaching, I was part of a group of teachers at larger art workshops like Squam and the Makerie. Also, I was invited by art studios and workshop spaces around the country to teach. There, I was the only teacher and the studio did most of the organizing. In all of these scenarios, I was paid a flat rate per student/per day. Nowadays, I choose where I want to go and find someone who can help with organizing and

creating the event. It's certainly more financially lucrative to do them on my own instead of being paid by the venue. I collect the money and then pay a fee to whomever organizes it for their service. I also run workshops out of my own space, Soul Shine Studio, in Portland, Oregon. Considering I have such a large audience of people who want to take the workshops, I can just announce the workshops on my website and they fill up right away. I'm very blessed like that!

What advice do you have for artists that are considering teaching as a source of income?

You really need to like people, have compassion, and be patient. And you need to be able to relate to different kinds of people—that translates well into teaching. I also think it's important to come from a place of generosity. You might worry if you teach certain techniques that people will copy you. If you choose the path of teacher, you have to be able to say, "I am giving this freely."

Teachers get a lot of the same questions over and over again, so you have to be incredibly patient. I also make it really clear to my students there is no possible way they can make a mistake. I do a lot to set the stage so people are comfortable and have a place to start. The very first thing I have them do is a blindfolded painting to a bad song. It's so much fun. People start to relax and get into the feeling of painting, instead of focusing on what it looks like.

With all the opportunities you have to teach or license your work, how do you decide what work to take on and what work to say no to?

My whole thing is intuition. I like to sit with stuff. Also, every year I come up with words that describe what I want for that year. So if an opportunity comes my way and it doesn't fit into my words for the year, I don't take it on. For example, this year is all about ease and collaboration and I'll say yes to things that fit with those words. I look back to what I've said yes to and can't believe what I took on. But I don't regret any of it because that's how we learn.

When you do feel overwhelmed and you are going through a particularly busy time, what do you do to stay focused and grounded?

I had a big realization that self-care, which for me is yoga, walks, and eating right, is not a luxury. It should be part of regular life because it's really important.

How do you approach the "left-brained" aspects of self-employment, like planning, bookkeeping, accounting, taxes, and billing?

I have a certain threshold where I enjoy those things, but I am a strong believer in hiring people to do things that you are either not good at or don't enjoy. It's extremely important to have your housekeeping (financial and otherwise) in order so that when you are in front of the canvas you can be free and wild. But that doesn't mean you have to do it all yourself.

LEARNING TO SAY NO

Every artist wants to get to the point where their work is in such demand that they can turn down opportunities. It's a sign of success when you can be picky about which commissions to take, galleries to work with, or illustration jobs to accept. And, yet, when they do get there, artists often have a hard time saying no. Why? You might be worried that the client or gallery will never come calling again or that it's the last opportunity you'll have in a long time. You might be worried about offending, sabotaging, or even being seen as lazy! As a result, artists often take on more than they can handle. In the end, you'll burn out and likely not deliver your highest-quality work.

When I find myself having a hard time saying no, I always remember a piece of advice someone gave me: "Saying no to one thing means saying yes to another." Indeed, saying no to one opportunity (especially those you are not excited about) opens up the space to say yes when another opportunity comes your way. It also creates free time to share with family, friends, and yourself!

Saying No Politely and Professionally

Saying no doesn't automatically mean a client or gallery will write you off forever. Whether you don't have enough time or it's just not the right fit, it's important to decline in a way that will not damage the relationship. First, reply promptly, just as quickly as if you were accepting the job. This sends the message that you appreciate that the client or gallery thought of you. And if you are declining because of time constraints, be explicit about how you would like another chance to work together in the future. And always, be polite and gracious by thanking them for the opportunity.

Create Criteria for Saying Yes

A few years ago, I had reached a pivotal point in my career where I was swimming in opportunity, but overwhelmed with how to handle all of it.

So I began working with a coach who helped me achieve more balance in my life. One of the things we worked on was developing criteria for saying yes when an opportunity came my way. We decided that three of my four criteria had to be met in order for me to say yes to an opportunity.

The criteria were:

1. The project is offering decent pay or potential for pay.

2. I have time in my schedule to complete the work.

3. The job would provide good exposure.

4. My aesthetic and values align with that of the client or gallery.

Developing your own criteria reflecting your own values, preferences, and goals can help you tremendously in making decisions. Of course, having criteria is not foolproof! There are always opportunities that come your way that don't fall neatly in the "work" category, but are time-consuming nonetheless, like press interviews and speaking engagements—so you may find yourself developing criteria for different situations.

HIRING HELP

It might just be seasonal or part-time, but hiring help can alleviate stress for busy artists. Since the actual work of making art is highly personal, it's often hard for artists to delegate studio work unless there is some production involved, which is more typical in sculpture and installation work. But if studio help won't benefit you, there are other ways you can parcel out portions of your workload. The first step is to consider all the things you spend time doing that take time away from making the actual artwork and can be handled by an assistant, like bookkeeping, invoicing, packing and shipping, and shopping for supplies.

The decision to hire someone shouldn't be made lightly because you'll be committing to paying them regularly. You'll have to determine what you can afford to pay an assistant and for how many hours a week. There are other considerations as well: Do you have enough space to house an assistant along with necessities like a computer or desk? Do you have time to plan your assistant's week in addition to your own? Once you've considered all of the challenges and are determined to hire an assistant, look for someone who is eager to learn from you. Most artist assistants are also creative and relish the chance to be inside the studio of a professional artist to learn from you. Hire someone who is not only enthusiastic about your work, but who also wants to engage in all aspects of the business, especially mundane ones like creating a press list, organizing your supplies, or even sweeping the studio floor. Consider a trial period before committing to make sure they are the right person for the job. Finding someone with experience should matter, but not nearly as much as bringing someone in with a positive attitude and enthusiasm.

 ## THE SIGNS OF TOO MUCH SUCCESS

It's not too hard to spot the signs of overworking: you feel tired, exhausted, and possibly anxious. You might even have trouble sleeping or focusing. Every person's bandwidth for how much work they can take on is different. Some artists are highly productive and thrive with multiple projects, while others feel overwhelmed with more than one illustration job at a time. Paying attention to the signs of stress and overwork can help you determine what's too much for you. When you notice these signs, it's important to stop and evaluate your current situation. Is this a temporary situation that you just need to get through? Or is this a larger problem? If you have reached your capacity, consider being more judicious about which jobs or commitments you say yes to so that you do not burn out. Maybe it's a matter of taking more breaks to recharge. Often, the simple act of taking a couple hours away from your worktable to nap, walk, eat, or exercise can alleviate exhaustion or lack of focus.

PAULA SCHER

Painter and graphic designer

NEW YORK, NEW YORK

WWW.PENTAGRAM.COM

In the early 1990s, artist Paula Scher painted the first in her now-famous series of map paintings—and it happened by accident. The award-winning graphic designer was asked to create the cover for an issue of the AIGA annual. She chose to paint a map of the United States by hand instead of using her usual graphic design tools. Because of the reception of that cover, she went on to produce scores of paintings of intricate, colorful typographic maps, both small and increasingly large. Paula has been a principal in the New York office of the design firm Pentagram since 1991. She began her career as an art director in the 1970s and has worked with clients like Public Theater, the Museum of Modern Art, Bloomberg, Citi, and Microsoft. Her work has been exhibited worldwide and is in the permanent collections of the Museum of Modern Art, the Victoria and Albert Museum, and the Centre Georges Pompidou, as well as many other institutions. Her teaching career includes over two decades at the School of Visual Arts, along with positions at the Cooper Union, Yale University, and the Tyler School of Art. She is the author of *Make It Bigger*, about graphic design, and *MAPS*, a monograph of her paintings.

Why did you choose to paint the cover of the AIGA annual?

AIGA offered no design fee for the cover, but they paid for design expenses, so I figured if I made everything by hand I could keep the expense money. I painted a humorous information-based cover with a map of the United States on the back. I actually left out Utah by accident, so I put it in the Pacific Ocean with an arrow. It became a popular cover, but more importantly for me, I began creating paintings of fractured information. I painted other informational diagrams and they evolved into maps. And they were small at first.

They were also opinionated maps. For example, I took a country in South America and instead of listing the cities, I wrote whether or not I thought there was drug traffic-king there. They were intentionally witty, snarky, and snide.

These early map paintings were put in a show and a collector bought them. I became encouraged, and I started making them big. But when I started to paint them at large scale, I began to realize that I was manipulating information. Originally the maps were deliberately fractured. They were illustrations through which I was commenting on things. When I started doing them bigger they changed. They weren't my own editorializing. Of course, they were in that I controlled the information, but the information was not overtly snide or political like in my earlier work. You made your own political assumptions about my maps by looking at the map, and more was left to the viewer.

How long does it take you to complete a large-scale painting? What is your painting process?

They take a long time (three to six months) because I don't paint full-time. I did one once when I was on a deadline and I painted it in about a month and a half. The experience was horrible! I felt like I was rushing and pressured. I had to stay in a room by myself for three weeks. You go crazy working like that.

When I begin, I have a general overall direction. When I first started making map paintings, they were very recognizable because they were defined by land masses. Compositionally you'd recognize the land masses, and then you'd see the information painted inside of them, what I call abstract expressionistic information. They created a feeling. My newer map paintings are much more about the pattern of cities and how infrastructures connect— rail systems, bus systems, road systems, and flight patterns. They don't have the same mass form as the old paintings. There are rivers that run through them but there are no outline borders that define them. I do think about what I'm going to paint in advance. I try to understand, for example, the systems in a city before I begin so I can add them in layers.

What is the inspiration behind your series of city paintings?

It all started with New York City. Over the years, I've done four paintings of New York City. I kept coming back to it because I liked the connections more than the form of the area. I thought it would be interesting to see if people would have the same emotional connection to the map with this layering of infrastructure as they would recognizing it as a specific shape. For example, I have one painting of London that is all layers and looks like a blob, and people do relate to it. I find that when people see one of my paintings of a place where they live, they want to buy it. People who buy my paintings have some emotional connection to the place.

How does your work as a graphic designer differentiate from your work as a painter?

As a graphic designer, the point is to communicate some specific message to the audience. My maps are not really like that anymore. You take what you want from them. The message isn't clear. With design, there is a clear objective of what the piece is supposed to accomplish or communicate for some purpose. In fine art you don't have the same goal. Graphic communication is resolved. Fine art is always unresolved. You begin to play with things in fine art; you ask questions, as opposed to answering questions or leading people to come to a particular viewpoint.

SLOWING DOWN AND ACHIEVING BALANCE

Despite all the efforts we make to manage our workloads with spreadsheets, delegating work to other people, and saying no to projects, we still may find that we work too much and making time for relaxation and balance has taken a backseat. The only thing that can remedy that is actually forcing yourself to take breaks from work—from fifteen-minute breaks in the middle of the day to days off every couple of weeks, or even taking entire weeks or months off to recharge. "I value big chunks of work time like gold. But if I need to just take a break and recharge, I will," says artist Kelly Tunstall. "There's no use in burning out as an artist—or as a partner or parent."

Achieving balance doesn't mean not working hard or not taking on more than a few projects at one time. Hardworking people can also lead balanced lives. It just means making sure you take adequate amounts of relaxation—taking walks, spending time with family, meditating, exercising, eating well, socializing with friends, and going on vacations. "I try to maintain a healthy schedule that includes downtime every day, otherwise I won't ever rest, and after a few days I am exhausted," says Michelle Armas. "When I am busy and have to make personal sacrifices, I plan a really fun outing to celebrate when I'm finished, so that I have something to look forward to, like a lunch, shopping, or chatting day with friends."

I like to think of work/life balance as a seesaw in a children's playground. The amount of time you spend working should be balanced with the amount of time you spend relaxing, resting, and pursuing other interests. Often it's when we are in periods of extreme stress that we most need to find balance. I find that taking regular yoga classes twice a week helps keep me grounded after long days of drawing. And just at the moment when I feel I'm beginning to lose focus on my work, I force myself to go outside and walk. Taking short breaks helps to regain perspective and focus. Simple things like eating healthy meals and getting eight hours of sleep go a long way toward helping manage stress.

ONWARD AND UPWARD

Success. What is great about this word is that you get to define it on your own terms. For some, success might be about recognition, fame, winning competitions, being represented by a prestigious gallery, or having a big collector base. For others, it may be much simpler. Success could mean making enough money to pay your bills or take care of your family, having your own studio space, or being in a group show. For most people, success is a combination of both high-level goals and smaller, basic goals. Success is also evolving; it may change over time as you reach goals and set your sights on new achievements or as your life changes with marriage or having kids. Each of us has a definition of success that includes accomplishments, relaxation, and relationships with other human beings.

Just because your work is in demand does not mean you are doomed to a life of only work and no play. Part of ensuring that your life does not become all about work is making decisions that reflect your real values and what makes you happy. At times, that means saying no to potential clients or gallery shows in favor of saying yes to a vacation with your family, or negotiating with clients to allow for more time to complete a project. It could also mean putting your Etsy shop on hiatus so you can focus all of your energy on completing work for a show. As artists, we can have enormous success, but we also have a responsibility to stay true to our values and our commitments to ourselves, our loved ones, and our families. Finding equanimity in the midst of our creative and entrepreneurial journeys is truly our life's work.

RESOURCES

Interviewees

Michelle Armas, www.michelle
armas.com
Flora Bowley, www.brave
intuitiveyou.com
Betsy Cordes, www.february13
creative.com
Claire Desjardins, www.claire
desjardins.com
Alyson Fox, www.alysonfox.com
Dolan Geiman, www.dolan
geiman.com
Susie Ghahremani, www.boygirl
party.com
Mark Hearld, www.markhearld
.co.uk
Josh Keyes, www.joshkeyes.net
Nikki McClure, www.nikki
mcclure.com
Shannon Rankin, www.artist
shannonrankin.com
Rebecca Rebouché, www.rebecca
rebouche.com
Eric Rewitzer and Annie Galvin,
www.3fishstudios.com
Paula Scher, www.pentagram.com
Julie Schneider, www.etsy.com
Jessica Silverman, www.jessica
silvermangallery.com
Lisa Solomon, www.lisasolomon
.com

Kelly Tunstall, www.kellytunstall
.com
Esther Pearl Watson, www.esther
pearlwatson.com

Administrative Tools

Freckle, www.letsfreckle.com
Google Apps, www.google.com/
apps
Harvest, www.getharvest.com
Hightail, www.hightail.com
Send6, www.send6.com
Skype, www.skype.com
WeTransfer, www.wetransfer.com

Blog Hosting

Blogger, www.blogger.com
Tumblr, www.tumblr.com
Typepad, www.typepad.com
Weebly, www.weebly.com
WordPress, www.wordpress.com

Call for Artists Sites

ArtPoints, www.artpoints.net/
calendar.html
Art Deadlines List, www.artdead
lineslist.com
The Art List, www.the-art-list.com
Art Show, www.artshow.com/
juriedshows
Artists Online, www.artistsonline
.com
California Arts Council, www
.cac.ca.gov/artistcall

Chicago Artists Resource, www
.chicagoartistsresource.org/
calls-for-artists

New York Foundation for the Arts,
www.nyfa.org/opportunities

Print Competitions and Annuals

American Illustration, www.ai-ap
.com

Communication Arts magazine,
www.commarts.com

New American Paintings, www
.newamericanpaintings.com

Workbook, www.workbook.com

Work/Life, www.uppercase
magazine.com

Financial Products and Services

FreshBooks, www.freshbooks.com

Kashoo, www.kashoo.com

Mint, www.mint.com

PayPal, www.paypal.com

ProPay, http://epay.propay.com

QuickBooks, http://quickbooks
.intuit.com

Sage (formerly Peachtree), http://
na.sage.com

Fine Art Reproduction Services

Fine Print Imaging, www.fine
printimaging.com

iolabs, www.iolabsinc.com

Photoworks, www.photoworkssf
.com

Picture Salon, www.picturesalon
.com

Wallblank, www.wallblank.com

Illustration Conferences

**The Illustration Conference
(ICON),** http://8.theillustration
conference.org

**Society of Children's Book Writers
and Illustrators Conference,**
www.scbwi.org

Art Licensing Trade Shows

The International Textile Show,
www.californiamarketcenter
.com/latextile

Printsource, www.printsource
newyork.com

Surtex, www.surtex.com

Email Marketing Services

Campaign Monitor, www
.campaignmonitor.com

Constant Contact, www
.constantcontact.com

MailChimp, www.mailchimp.com

Online Shop Venues and Platforms

Big Cartel, www.bigcartel.com
Cargoh, www.cargoh.com
Etsy, www.etsy.com
Imagekind, www.imagekind.com
Saatchi Online, www.saatchi online.com
Shopify, www.shopify.com
Society6, www.society6.com

Printing Services

Got Print, www.gotprint.com
Juke Box Print, www.jukeboxprint .com
Moo, www.moo.com
Overnight Prints, www.overnight prints.com
Scout Books, www.scoutbooks .com
Vistaprint, www.vistaprint.com

Professional Organizations

Art Directors Club, www.adc global.org
The Association of Illustrators, www.theaoi.com
Freelancers Union, www .freelancersunion.org
The Illustrators' Partnership of America, www.illustrators partnership.org

National Association of Independent Artists, www.naia-artists .org
National Endowment for the Arts, www.arts.gov
Society of Illustrators, www .societyillustrators.org

Protecting Your Work

Creative Commons, www .creativecommons.org
U.S. Copyright Office, www .copyright.gov
U.S. Patent and Trademark Office, www.uspto.gov

Residencies

18th Street Arts Center, www.18thstreet.org
Adolf Konrad, Newark Museum Arts Workshop, www.newark museum.org
Atlantic Center for the Arts, www .atlanticcenterforthearts.org
Bemis Center for Contemporary Art, www.bemiscenter.org
Chinati Foundation, www.chinati .org
The Edward F. Albee Foundation, www.albeefoundation.org
Fire Island Artist Residency, www .fireislandartistresidency.org

Headlands Center for the Arts, www.headlands.org

Kansas City International Residency Program, www.kansascityartistscoalition.org

MacDowell Colony, www.macdowellcolony.org

National Park Service Residencies, www.nps.gov/getinvolved/artist-in-residence.htm

Ox-Bow, www.ox-bow.org

Skowhegan School of Painting and Sculpture, www.skowheganart.org

Smack Mellon, www.smackmellon.org

Studio Museum in Harlem, www.studiomuseum.org

Vermont Studio Center, www.vermontstudiocenter.org

Small Business Assistance

Companies Incorporated, www.companiesinc.com

Nolo, www.nolo.com

U.S. Small Business Administration, www.sba.gov

Tax Information

U.S. Internal Revenue Service, www.irs.gov

Website Publishing, Domains, and Hosting

4ormat, www.4ormat.com

Adobe Muse, www.muse-themes.com

Cargo Collective, www.cargocollective.com

GoDaddy, www.godaddy.com

icompendium, www.icompendium.com

Network Solutions, www.networksolutions.com

SiteGround, www.siteground.com

Squarespace, www.squarespace.com

Virb, www.virb.com

Weebly, www.weebly.com

WordPress, www.wordpress.com

INDEX

ACKNOWLEDGMENTS

First and foremost, I would like to thank Meg Mateo Ilasco, without whom this book would never have been possible. Your vision for this book, your faith in me, your meticulous editing, and your steadfast and patient mentorship have not only made this book what it is, but also made me a better writer. I could not have done this without you! Thank you to my editors, Kate Woodrow and Caitlin Kirkpatrick, for your positive guidance, ever-thoughtful feedback, and constant encouragement. To my literary agent, Stefanie Von Borstel, for helping me to connect all the dots in my new endeavor as a writer. To Karolin Schnoor, for your stunning illustrations. To Emily Proud, for the time and energy you so enthusiastically gave to helping me with this project. To all of the brilliant and inspiring artists, agents, and gallery owners who took time out of their busy schedules to be interviewed for this book, and for sharing your experience and knowledge. To Jonathan Fields, my foreword writer, for your infinite wisdom and contagious enthusiasm. Last, to my wife, Clay Lauren Walsh, for your undying love and support as I undertook this project—thank you for making sure I ate and slept and showered amid the deadlines!